man who doubled as a dusty old guy named Buffalo Nichols every morning?

Today, we can be nostalgic about the passing of great local children's fare such as *Bozo's Circus, Ray Rayner and His Friends,* and *Garfield Goose.* However, I believe that today's children have more and better choices in programming via countless cable networks, PBS, and some broadcast offerings. What is missing is the localism, the heart and soul that emanated from these and other programs. Economics, regulation, and expectations for what a program should look like have altered children's television forever.

As you read through the chapters of this book, perhaps you will not only find memories or curiosities from a bygone era, but inspiration to create children's television for today's audiences. A pie in the face is still funny, kids still like to dance, and the last time I looked, you could still buy six buckets and nail them to a board and call it a Grand Prize Game.

Acknowledgments

Most books are collaborative endeavors, and this one is certainly no exception.

To cover this subject in the manner it deserves, we relied heavily upon the memories of those who were actually a part of this vital history. We are greatly indebted to the individuals who graciously shared their stories with us: Bruce Ballard, Marshall Brodien, Angel Casey, John Conrad, Dr. Lester Fisher, Allen Hall, Mary Hartline, Dick Hutter, Bill Jackson, Newton N. Minow, Elaine Mulqueen, Bruce and Claire Newton, Don Sandburg, Don Sanders, Emil Sitka, and Richard W. Tillstrom. Without their input, this book would not exist.

Sadly, some key figures of the era are no longer with us. Fortunately, interviews conducted by radio personalities Ed Schwartz and Dean Richards, columnists Deborah Dowley Preiser and Eric Zorn, and TV historians Cary O'Dell and George Pappas have preserved a lot of valuable information. Fan-historian Jerry Webb's incredible memory also helped to fill some major gaps in our research.

Writers need plenty of encouragement, especially during those bleak periods when the blank manuscript pages outnumber the completed ones. For their kind words, moral support, and willingness to surf the Internet for some elusive factoid, we would like to thank Vici Bielski, Jerry Broadsky, Jamie Brotherton, John Cavallo, Dennis Corpus, Chuck D'Alessio, Jason Dummeldinger, Bob Furmanek, David

J. Hogan, Bruce Ingram, Joe Konrath, Scott and Jan MacGillivray, David L. Miller, Mark A. Miller, James L. Neibaur, the Okuda family (Sakiko, Belinda, Cheryl, and Christopher), Eve Pool, Maureen and Victor Rothstein (Joe and Jackson, too!), Samuel K. Rubin, Ralph Schiller, Kathy Schultz, Kathryn Seckman, Karen Stanley, Larry Urbanski, and Bill Zehme.

We are indebted to Bruce DuMont of Chicago's Museum of Broadcast Communications and Neal Sabin of wcIU-Tv, Channel 26, for writing for the Introduction and Foreword, respectively.

We commend Sharon Woodhouse and Karen Formanski of Lake Claremont Press for their encouragement of this project from the very beginning. They provided the much-needed light at the end of our literary tunnel.

Our appreciation to Mary Deborah Englund, who took time out of her busy schedule to look over the text, and made many trenchant suggestions and corrections.

Thanks are also due to Marlena Bielski for her expert proofreading skills and knowledge of Chicago locales.

Our gratitude to Nathaniel Koch for access to his computer terminal (the apartment key is under the mat), with able technical assistance from Ryan "Age of Empires" Reynolds and Jerry "Civilization" King. And thanks to Miyk Camacho of Tower Records for access to his treasured printer.

And special praise to three helpful friends, all of them experts on the subject of Chicago children's television programming:

Jim Mueller has written numerous articles for the *Chicago Tribune* and other publications. When Jim covers a subject, it's as incisive and thorough as it gets, so it's no surprise that he made some valuable editorial suggestions. His expertise is exceeded only by his generosity.

David Maska is the kind of a person who gives 110 percent whenever anyone needs his assistance. His continuous phone calls, letters, and FedEx packages are proof of his dedication to our project. David provided us with so much information that giving him the praise he fully deserves would require a separate book entirely.

Acknowledgments

Mark Yurkiw is, without question, a leading authority on Chicago children's television. In an overwhelming gesture of generosity, Mark gave us complete access to his collection of interviews, articles, and other rare research material. He's destined to write a book of his own . . . that is, if he can ever find the time. (When he's not writing columns for the Riverside-Brookfield Landmark newspaper, Mark is a member of the improvisational comedy troupe Happy Clams and a writer-performer for the cable access program *The Funny Show*.) But he will be heard from; this we guarantee.

To all these fine folks, we give our eternal gratitude. (Sadly, Nathaniel Koch passed away before the publication of this book. He will be missed by his many friends.)

A Historical Overview

*Chicago had more good kid shows than anywhere
else in America. The shows were very different and the
people who did the shows were all very talented. This
city was so blessed.*
— Bill Jackson (*The B.J. and Dirty Dragon
Show, Cartoon Town, Gigglesnort Hotel*)

Two decades seemed to go by in a flash. Two decades
of puppets, clowns, pantomimes, songs, audience-participation games,
cartoons, and trips to the zoo.

The period from the late 1940s through the mid-1970s marked the
heyday, the golden age, of local children's programming in Chicago.
While New York and Los Angeles stations produced a good number of
kid shows, Chicago tackled the field with greater energy and ambition.
Al Hall, who directed and later produced the Chicago edition of *Bozo's
Circus*, observes, "Chicago was a unique market in that they had to
develop a lot of their own programming because the network services
in those early days was not as complete as it is now. Network service

was somewhat limited. It didn't go 24/7, so stations had to provide some kind of programming and the kids' audience was a good, viable audience at that time."

During the late 1940s, licenses for television stations were issued by the Federal Communications Commission (FCC). Since Channel 1 was—and still is—used by the military, stations could broadcast their shows on Channels 2 through 13 at very high frequency (VHF).

WBKB–Channel 4, the Chicago CBS affiliate, got things started in 1947 with *Junior Jamboree*, which introduced TV viewers to Burr Tillstrom, Fran Allison, and two puppets named Kukla and Ollie. The following year, the show's title was changed to *Kukla, Fran & Ollie*, a program still regarded as one of the high-water marks in television history.

The success of *Kukla, Fran & Ollie* prompted WBKB to produce additional children's fare, but most of these shows lacked the appeal of Tillstrom's offering. Shows like *Wrangler's Club* (1950), *Junior Rodeo* (1952), and *Silhouettes of the West* (1952) disappeared shortly after their debuts. However, the station did score with *The Play House* (1951–56) and *The Happy Pirates* (1952–56) and in 1952 introduced *Garfield*

◀ *Fran Allison (of* Kukla, Fran & Ollie*) chats with Jack Mulqueen's puppets on* WMAQ-TV *show* Bob & Kay *in 1955. (Courtesy of Jerry Broadsky.)*

and I think rightfully so. But as a result of the backlash, many children's shows disappeared. The sponsors didn't want to be bothered with financing stuff that was going to get them into trouble, and the stations didn't want to have something that was going to give them problems. I always thought WGN got a bad shot at that because, in my opinion, our guys always had a great respect for their audience."

The biggest blow to local kid shows came on January 1, 1972, when the NAB, under pressure from the FCC, ruled that kid show hosts could no longer present the sponsor's commercials. "What that meant," says Mulqueen, "was that you couldn't make the commercials part of the actual show anymore, nor could you give the products away to the studio audience. Sponsors have always felt that having a host do the commercial was a strong part of their participation on the program. When Bozo the Clown [Bob Bell] would do the McDonald's commercials, he'd form his hands and arms into the shape of the 'Golden Arches.' Coca-Cola felt that Pandora [Elaine Mulqueen] and the puppets on

▼ *Marvin the Lion (puppeteer Jack Mulqueen) and Pandora (Elaine Mulqueen) pose with Bozo (Bob Bell). The Mulqueens appeared weekly on* Bozo's Circus *from 1962 to 1963. (From the Mulqueen archives.)*

The Mulqueens stood a better chance of selling their product than some nondescript announcer. And with this ruling, hosts could no longer make personal appearances at food stores or sponsor-related public events."

Hall adds, "As a result of that ruling, the people who appeared on the shows could not appear in the commercials. On *Bozo's Circus*, we had to be careful regarding prizes. We couldn't give a product away that was being used in a commercial."

As sponsors stopped advertising, the lost revenue resulted in the cancellation of numerous kid shows. Accordingly, stations no longer had any interest in developing locally produced children's programming. Some shows were able to weather the storm and continue on in a different capacity, but for all intents and purposes, the golden age of Chicago children's television was over by 1974.

Ray Rayner (*Ray Rayner and His Friends, Bozo's Circus*) would later comment to writer Deborah Dowley Preiser, "When local performers could no longer set up a table and promote a product, a huge source of revenue evaporated. In a major market like Chicago, we had enough national sponsors to keep going. But programs in smaller markets depended on advertising from a large number of local stores."

Marshall Brodien (*Bozo's Circus*) remarked to radio personality Ed Schwartz, "One of the biggest things that hurt the children's shows are the restrictions that the NAB code has put on commercials. They say, 'You can't say this, you can't say that.' If you do a magic trick and say, 'I'm going to make it disappear,' they say, 'You don't make it disappear. You've got to say you *appear* to make it disappear.' I know a lot of companies that have gone off children's shows. And when [the stations] can't sell commercials on the shows, they won't run the shows."

Frazier Thomas (*Garfield Goose and Friends, Bozo's Circus*) added, "Children's shows have fallen on hard times, there's no question about that. Sponsors got afraid to get on children's shows; they shied away from them. As a result, the bosses look at this and say, 'Hey, we can't sell this thing—it costs too much to put this on.' [Anyone] who wants to keep his job is going to do what he thinks is right for his business or his station. Whether the end result is really what it ought to be, I would question that."

▲ TV *guide ads show the popularity of "Kiddie Prime Time." (From the collection of Ted Okuda.)*

So, with additional rules and regulations, has children's programming really improved? On May 9, 1991, exactly 20 years after he gave his "Vast Wasteland" speech, Newton N. Minow addressed the Freedom Forum Media Studies Center at Columbia University with a speech titled "How Vast the Wasteland Now?", in which he noted there was still a need for television to fulfill its potential for young viewers. Minow says today:

> I don't think the issues have changed. In a free society, where we don't have the government censoring broadcasters—and we shouldn't want that—we really have counted on broadcasters themselves to have a high sense of public purpose and serve the public interest. In respect to children's television, there's certainly been an expansion of choice, in the sense that channels like Nickelodeon didn't exist before, and public television has

devoted a lot of attention to children's programming. But most of commercial television has not and I think that's wrong.

With all the additional channels you have now, you still have the same problems, only multiplied. If I could change anything about children's programming today, I would set out terms of getting a broadcast license or a cable license, and I'd spell it out in advance. The terms would require a specified amount of time for children's programs with no commercials. The law uses the term "public interest" and everybody argues about what it means. I would say the public interest definitely means service to children and service to the democratic process. Those two things are not debatable.

Hall notes, "Well, there's fewer network children's shows, that's for sure. Nowadays, the major networks carry a bare minimum—the three hours they are required to carry by the FCC and that's it. The reason for that is they can sell their commercial time to a 'regular' advertiser."

Perhaps it's better for us to remember the past rather than try to live in it. In 1990, when asked to compare contemporary children's television with the golden age shows, Ned Locke (*Bozo's Circus, Lunchtime Little Theater*) told Deborah Dowley Preiser, "I don't think there's any comparison. You can't go back. Buick, for instance, may have made a good car in 1950. But that doesn't mean they should make the same car again. It's a whole different world now. Just like everything else, television has changed, too."

RATINGS FOR SATURDAY DECEMBER 8, 1963
TIME PERIOD: 9 A.M.
TV SETS OPERATING: 17 PERCENT

	Share	Percent	Households	Children
WBBM: *Quick Draw McGraw*	5	44	120,000	148,000
WMAQ: *Hector Heathcoat*	2	21	56,000	56,000
WBKB: *Safariland*	1	10	34,000	none
WGN: *The Mulqueens*	4	29	83,800	185,000

RATINGS MONDAY THROUGH FRIDAY
DECEMBER 1964
TIME PERIOD: NOON
TV SETS OPERATING: 24 PERCENT

	Share	Percent	Households	Children
WGN: *Bozo's Circus*	10	40	221,000	366,000
WBBM: *Noon Report*	9	39	215,000	18,000
WBKB: *The Rebus Game*	2	7	39,000	12,000
WMAQ: *Everything Relative*	4	15	84,000	18,000

Bozo's Circus and *Garfield Goose and Friends* were two programs that never had competition from other children's shows during their weekday time slots. The result was a huge kids' viewership. WGN had captured the family market without much of a fight.

As the following indicates, competing stations were using afternoons to fill time with movies, news reports, and reruns, while *Garfield Goose* was the only kid show offering.

MONDAY THROUGH FRIDAY RATINGS INDEX, DECEMBER 1964				
	Share	Percent	Households	Children
WBBM: *The Early Show*	6	21	266,000	78,000
WBKB: *The Big Show* (movies)	6	20	231,000	80,000
WMAQ: *The Rifleman*	6	21	281,000	76,000
WGN: *Garfield Goose*	12	40	664,000	587,000

But as soon as the baseball season started, *Garfield Goose* was regularly preempted, resulting in a drop-off in viewership.

	Share	Percent	Households	Children
MONDAY THROUGH FRIDAY **RATINGS INDEX, APRIL 1965**				
WBBM: *The Early Show*	5	26	112,000	44,000
WBKB: *The Big Show*	4	24	99,000	46,000
WMAQ: *Have Gun, Will Travel*	4	21	91,000	12,000
WGN: *Garfield Goose/Baseball*	5	27	237,000	201,000

By 1967 the viewing habits of the greater Chicagoland-area public had been changed with the introduction of UHF television. WCIU (Channel 26) was the first UHF station in Chicago. It was not just simply one more channel, because you had to purchase a television set that was equipped to handle the new signal. Another problem with UHF in those days was that it had a dial similar to a radio, instead of a click-on that would lock in the station signal. As a result, if the station's broadcast signal wasn't powerful enough, you could spend a great deal of time just trying to tune in the channel. WCIU had a strong signal for the western section of Chicago and the suburbs, but if you lived along Lake Michigan or in the Wisconsin suburbs, you weren't able to see anything.

WFLD (Channel 32), a rival UHF station, added to WCIU's problems. WFLD's signal was so powerful that its broadcasts were coming in clear—and in color! Kids who wanted to watch WCIU programming first had to struggle to get an image, and if they finally got one, it was black-and-white.

With so many areas in the Chicago market that couldn't get WCIU's signals, ARB and A.C. Nielsen could not get accurate ratings for the station. In fact, there was a time when Nielsen refused to acknowledge that WCIU had *any* viewing audience.

But ratings also reflected that *The Mulqueens' Kiddie-A-Go-Go* was tough competition for other networks in the same time period.

RATINGS MARCH THROUGH APRIL 1966				
	Share	**Percent**	**Households**	**Viewers**
WBBM: *Tennessee Tuxedo*	4	20	100,300	191,900
WMAQ: *Atom Ant*	6	30	144,500	252,300
WBKB: *The Mulqueens' Kiddie-A-Go-Go*	5	25	105,100	247,600
WGN: *The Three Stooges Show*	5	25	116,400	240,000

If a station discovers a program has low ratings, it can move the show to a different time slot, make talent changes, revise the format, and try to ride out the ratings battle. Sooner or later, if ratings don't improve, the station is forced to cancel the show and replace it with one that will hopefully perform better. That's why reruns of prime-time shows are so popular with local stations. These national programs come into a local market with an established track record, and even if they only pull in a fraction of the viewers that watched them the first time around, the numbers will still be big enough to be considered a success.

Then again, when *Kiddie-A-Go-Go* was on WBKB, drawing 247,600 viewers, we learned the hard way that if station managers did not want your show, ratings simply didn't matter. If they wanted you gone, you were gone, regardless of the numbers. It truly was a ratings *game.*

4 | The Puppet Master
Burr Tillstrom and Kukla, Fran and Ollie

Burr Tillstrom was an inspiration to me and a heck of a lot of other people.
— Muppets creator Jim Henson

Burr made my life important. He wanted to make life important for everyone.
— Fran Allison

I hope it doesn't sound too holy, but we loved our audience and they loved us. [The show] was just a big love affair.
— Burr Tillstrom

Few children's television shows—few television shows in general, for that matter—made an impact on the medium like *Kukla, Fran & Ollie*. With puppeteer Burr Tillstrom as its guiding force, the program appealed to everyone because it was never specifically targeted at a young audience. His older brother, Richard Tillstrom, remembers, "It wasn't just a kids' program, it was actually a family-oriented program. It finally got categorized as children's programming, which is fine, but it really dealt with day-to-day family life."

"Burr never thought that he was doing children's programs," observes former FCC Chairman Newton N. Minow. "He wanted the entire family to watch and he was very often being understood at different levels. Burr was an enormous talent and he had a great sense of not only entertainment but values."

Born in Chicago on October 13, 1917, Burr Tillstrom displayed a creative bent at an early age. Richard Tillstrom recalls, "As kids, we used to have these little lead soldiers and we'd make miniature battlefields, putting small firecrackers into little cannons. We thought that was great stuff. Burr was also into marionettes. Tony Sarg, a famous puppeteer from way back, was a big influence on him. In fact, at one time, Tony's sister lived across the street from us while we were growing up in the Glenwood and Granville area of Chicago. When he was just a young child, Burr would use teddy bears to put on puppet shows for the family."

Burr earned a scholarship while attending the University of Chicago. After a year there, he quit school and joined the WPA (Works Progress Administration) Park Project, putting on various puppet shows in the Chicago area. "I had never been acquainted with hand puppets before," he later told writer Gary H. Grossman. "The director of the group suggested we all try to make some hand puppets, and I decided that when I finished mine I would give it to a friend who had given great advice. When I had [the puppet] all ready to go, he looked so beautiful. I really loved him, so I asked my mother what I should do. She said keep him and make another for a gift."

Shortly thereafter, in the fall of 1936, Burr, who also had a great interest in ballet, went backstage at Chicago's Auditorium Theater to visit one of his idols, Ballet Russe dancer Tamara Toumanova. While she was sitting in front of her makeup mirror, Tillstrom placed his puppet on her shoulder. Delighted, she exclaimed, "Kukla!," a Russian term for "doll." And so the first of several Tillstrom characters was born. A year later, Tillstrom created Oliver J. Dragon, who would be Kukla's odd-couple partner for the rest of his career.

If being in the right place at the right time is the key to success, then Burr Tillstrom was a roaring success at the ripe old age of 21. In 1939, while working in the toy department and staging puppet shows at the Marshall Field's department store in downtown Chicago, Burr saw an RCA Victor demonstration of television broadcasting. Richard Tillstrom relates, "Burr asked one of the engineers in charge of the

▶ *Puppets Kukla and Ollie of* Kukla, Fran & Ollie *(puppeteer Burr Tillstrom). (Courtesy of the Burr Tillstrom Copyright Trust, Richard Tillstrom Trustee.)*

demonstration if he could get his puppet on camera, and the guy said, 'Yeah, sure, we'll put him on.'" Garry Moore, host of the radio program *Club Matinee*, was in front of the camera; Burr stepped behind a makeshift stage. As Moore interacted with Kukla, their images were being broadcast over closed-circuit TV.

Burr was immediately hooked on the new medium. Richard Tillstrom remembers, "He was so excited about television. He said, 'This is what I want to do! Think of all the people I can reach and what fun it will be. It's wonderful!'"

RCA thought he was wonderful, too, and invited Burr and his puppets to participate in their television exhibit at the 1939 New York World's Fair. In 1941 Burr, Kukla, and Ollie were part of the very first television broadcasts of WBKB, the Chicago station that would later launch his first program.

At the outbreak of World War II, Burr tried to enlist in the service but was turned down because he had flat feet. Still wanting to contribute to the war effort, he put on puppet shows to help sell defense bonds. It was during this period that Tillstrom first encountered Fran Allison, whose name would be forever linked with his. Allison, a former schoolteacher, was a regular cast member on the radio show *Don McNeill's Breakfast Club*, playing a character named Aunt Fanny. She joined Burr and his puppets for a bond rally in front of the Wrigley Building at the Michigan Avenue bridge. Since they had never worked together before, there was no set routine, so they just ad-libbed their dialogue. When Kukla innocently asked Fran for a kiss, she closed her eyes in anticipation of receiving a peck from the puppet and was surprised when Burr delivered the kiss himself. It was, as the old saying goes, the beginning of a beautiful friendship.

In 1947 RCA Victor approached Tillstrom about doing a television show for its Chicago station, WBKB. While preparing for the program, Burr realized he couldn't work with a script because he couldn't turn the pages when he was handling the puppets (Kukla was always on his right hand, Ollie on his left). He decided that ad-libbing was the only solution and knew that he would need a like-minded performer to work with. Fran Allison was his first and only choice. As Tillstrom later commented, "You don't need a script when you're talking to your friends."

Junior Jamboree, as the program was originally titled, debuted on October 13, 1947, Burr's 30th birthday. It was an amazing achievement. Tillstrom's puppet creations, dubbed the Kuklapolitan Players, immediately captured the hearts and the imaginations of early television viewers. There was Kukla, a bald, bulb-nosed, rosy-cheeked, mild-mannered little clownlike figure who never seemed fully at ease with the things going on around him. His eyebrows were always arched, and his mouth formed a perpetual "O" shape, as if he were in a constant state of surprise. Single-toothed Oliver J. Dragon — Ollie to his associates — was outgoing and outspoken, never passing up the opportunity to say exactly what was on his mind at any given moment. Tillstrom provided Ollie with a detailed background: Ollie's great-great-great-great-grandfather had swallowed some water while swimming the Hellespont, so he came from a long line of non–fire-breathing dragons. He also hailed from Vermont, where his parents operated Dragon Retreat.

Other Kuklapolitans included droopy-eared mail carrier Fletcher Rabbit, who starched his ears for formal occasions and often spoke of his suffragette mother; Buelah Witch (her moniker derived from a varied spelling of producer Beulah Zachary's first name), who rode around on a jet-propelled broomstick; Madame Ophelia Ooglepuss, a former opera singer; Southern gentleman Colonel Crackie; Mercedes, the company ingenue; stage manager Cecil Bill, a former sailor; Clara Coo Coo; Paul Pookenschlagl; and members of Ollie's family: mother Olivia and sister Dolores.

Richard Tillstrom comments:

> A lot of people never realized Burr did all the puppet voices himself. He had a real talent for voices. There were times when he could make it sound as though several puppets were talking or singing all at the same time.
>
> Of all the characters, I guess Kukla was the closest to the kind of person Burr was: a gentle, nice guy. He used to claim that he could say things through Ollie that he'd never dream of saying himself, because Ollie was a little pushy and headstrong, and could get away with more.

As entertaining as these creations were, the heart of the show was their interaction with Fran Allison, the only live person in front of the cameras. Fran would later remark, "Working with Burr was a meeting

▶ *Fran Allison and Burr Tillstrom publicity photo for* Kukla, Fran & Ollie, *which was shown locally and nationally over* ABC *and* NBC *networks, 1948–1954. (Photos on pages 35–41 courtesy of the Burr Tillstrom Copyright Trust, Richard Tillstrom Trustee.)*

▲ *Burr Tillstrom and Kukla of* Kukla, Fran & Ollie

▲ *Fran Allison of* Kukla, Fran & Ollie

of minds. And the puppets were so real to me that I related to them as real people."

"Fran was a dear, sweet, wonderful person," says Richard Tillstrom. "She and my brother had a rapport and affection that really made the show work. Fran looked upon those puppets as real. She never wanted to see them anywhere but onstage; she couldn't bear the idea of them hanging on a hook or stuffed in a box."

Burr and Fran's improvised dialogue and reactions gave the show a spontaneous feeling that was rare, even for early television. "I would watch from behind the scenes when they first went on," says Richard Tillstrom. "They never had any lines to memorize. Before each show, they'd discuss a plan, then they'd ad-lib according to what they had worked out."

Which is not to imply that everything was up for grabs. Thanks to musical director Jack Fascinato, the show presented some surprising musical interludes, from a simple song ("Lemonade") to parodies (*Martin Dragon, Private Tooth*) to Gilbert and Sullivan operettas (*The Mikado* with Kukla as Nanki Poo, Fran as Yum Yum, and Ollie as the

Lord High Executioner). In 1953 NBC aired the Kuklapolitan version of *St. George and the Dragon* as one of the network's first experimental color broadcasts.

From the very start, the show struck an emotional chord with its audience. During the debut week, Kukla blew his nose on a curtain, and 250 viewers sent handkerchiefs to the studio. As Tillstrom related to Gary H. Grossman, "When the handkerchiefs came in, I knew there were viewers out there who cared. And I realized the awesome truth that I was affecting people's minds, thoughts, and feelings." In time, the ranks of Kuklapolitan admirers would include Katharine Hepburn, Judy Garland, Marlon Brando, John Steinbeck, and Lillian and Dorothy Gish.

The show's popularity resulted in some establishments making special arrangements for younger viewers. Richard Tillstrom recalls, "When the show first went on the air, a lot of people didn't have television sets, but most barrooms did. So some of the barroom owners would invite the public to bring their kids down to watch this puppet show. I thought it was pretty darn good of them to do that."

By November 1948, the show had been rechristened *Kukla, Fran & Ollie* and was broadcast on NBC's Midwest network. Thanks to coaxial cable, it was fed to the East Coast in January 1949, and by 1951 it was

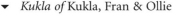
▼ *Kukla of* Kukla, Fran & Ollie

▲ *Ollie of* Kukla, Fran & Ollie

◀ *Paul Pookenschlagl*
of Kukla, Fran & Ollie

▲ *Colonel Crackie of*
Kukla, Fran & Ollie

◀ *Fletcher Rabbit of*
Kukla, Fran & Ollie

shown live on the West Coast as well. In addition to their own program, Burr & Co. also made guest appearances on *The Today Show, Your Show of Shows,* and *Your Hit Parade.*

By the early 1950s, Richard Tillstrom had moved to Grand Rapids, Michigan, where he embarked on his own children's program.

> I was doing puppet shows for hospitals and supermarket openings, just as a sideline. The program director for WOOD-TV took his kid to see one of these shows, and called me the next day to see if I'd be interested in putting together a TV show for his station. That's how I wound up doing *Westward Ho Ho* [1952–1955], a puppet show about these city hicks who inherit a ranch out west. Like Burr's program, it was all ad-lib. After it went off the air, I got into the administrative end of things.

▶ *Mercedes of* Kukla, Fran & Ollie

▶ *Buelah Witch of* Kukla, Fran & Ollie

▲ *Cecil Bill of* Kukla, Fran & Ollie

While I was at woo d, Ray Rayner had a weather show called *Rayner Shine*. He was a nice guy and of course you know he had a lengthy career in children's programming himself.

(For more on Rayner, see Chapter 7.)

Kukla, Fran & Ollie was still riding a wave of popularity when NBC made the fateful decision to trim the show's running time. Beginning Monday, November 21, 1951, Tillstrom's daily 30-minute program was sliced in half, with the other 15 minutes devoted to comedians Bob and Ray (Bob Elliott and Ray Goulding). While the decision outraged fans and critics, Tillstrom poked fun at the situation on the first 15-minute telecast by having Ollie request that everyone talk faster so they wouldn't exceed their allotted time. (Tillstrom even shortened his named to Burtlestrom in the show's credits.)

No amount of fan pleading or editorial backlash seemed to alter the network's decision. On August 25, 1952, *Kukla, Fran & Ollie* left the weekday schedule entirely and was given a Sunday afternoon time slot. Two years later, on June 13, 1954, the show had its last NBC broadcast.

The show wound up on the ABC network on September 6, 1954, still in a 15-minute broadcast. It ran for another three years, coming to an end on August 30, 1957. "There's no place in TV for us anymore," Tillstrom said at the time. "The industry has gotten too used to us. They've taken us for granted. People in TV would rather make money than provide entertainment."

Yet someone with Tillstrom's imagination and creative gifts could not remain idle for very long. He was involved in the coverage of the 1960 presidential election on *The Today Show*. His puppetry was a regular feature on *That Was the Week That Was* (1964–65), NBC's groundbreaking satiric revue. For the show, he devised a "Berlin Wall Hand Ballet," using his bare hands to express the heartbreak caused by the recently constructed wall; he won an Emmy Award for his efforts.

Tillstrom and Fran Allison would again join forces for other Kukla, Fran & Ollie projects: a five-minute weekday spot on NBC (1961–62); on PBS (1969–71), winning an Emmy Award in 1971; and hosting the *CBS Children's Film Festival* on Saturdays (1967) and a syndicated series (1975–76). They also reteamed in the 1980s for specials like "Happy Birthday, Buelah Witch!" and "'Tis the Season to Be Ollie." From 1979 to 1984, they performed Christmas shows at Chicago's Goodman Theatre.

"Burr and Fran were terrific people," remembers Jack Mulqueen. "In the late 1950s, I was scheduled to appear with my puppets on a local NBC show called *Bob and Kaye* with Bob Murphy and Kay Westfall. Kay wound up taking the day off and Fran Allison was asked to fill in for her. Bob wanted to cancel my appearance, claiming that Fran would never agree to work with another puppeteer. I took it upon myself to call Fran directly and found her to be very agreeable. She wound up appearing with me, and, thanks to her, the skit went over extremely well. Later, Fran invited me to see Burr perform, and all of us got along so well."

▶ *Madame Ooglepuss of*
Kukla, Fran & Ollie

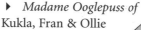

◀ *Dolores Dragon of* Kukla,
Fran & Ollie

"Burr was very helpful to others," says Richard Tillstrom. "I know he gave advice to Shari Lewis. When Burr was living in New York City, he was in the same building—on Beakman Place—in which Jim Henson and his wife Jane were living. He got to know Jim and gave him a lot of encouragement."

Burr Tillstrom died on December 6, 1985. His story is also the story of the birth of television. His work was distinguished by a gentility and grace that are still rare to find.

"My brother was an innovator," remarks Richard Tillstrom. "And yet he took it all in stride. He never looked at his career from that angle. He was rather modest about it, actually. He was just very grateful for his success and enjoyed every bit of it."

acts: trained elephants, bears, chimps, and dogs were paraded across the stage; trapeze artists swung from the rafters; and acrobats bounced on trampolines or teetered on balance beams. All this plus a relentless stream of commercial pitches hawking everything from Canada Dry Ginger Ale to Kellogg's cereals. (The young studio audience was encouraged to bellow "Kellogg's!" whenever they were asked, "What is the greatest name in cereal?")

Aiding and abetting Mary were ringmaster Claude Kirchner (a former carnival barker, Kirchner was pitch-perfect for the role) and a trio of talented clowns: Cliffy Sobier, Nicky Francis, and Bardy Patton, son of *Super Circus* producer Phil Patton. (Sandy Dobritch later replaced Bardy Patton.)

But it was Mary Hartline, the beguiling bandleader guiding the bigtop tempo, who received the most media attention. Her musical technique was spirited, to put it mildly, as she would energetically conduct a lively band number, usually her theme song, Jerome Kern's "Who (Stole My Heart Away)?" She was also peppy and engaging with the awestruck children who were called onstage to participate in games. These contestants were selected by the Super Seeker, a bouncing arrow superimposed over shots of the audience. (*Bozo's Circus* later used a similar Magic Arrows device.)

Hartline became one of TV's first idols, setting off a merchandising craze of dolls, clothing, comic books, coloring books, record albums, and other paraphernalia. Her picture regularly appeared on the covers of television guides and national magazines. Many honorary titles were bestowed upon her, including "Sweetest Star of Television" and "Chicago's Number One Career Girl." In 1950 she vacationed in Hollywood, and the press reported she was showered with screen test offers, which she rejected in favor of returning to Chicago.

Mary's success resulted in her starring in another children's program, *The Mary Hartline Show*, which debuted in 1951. This half-hour daily local show aired at 5 P.M. on WENR and featured Mary and her piano-playing cohort Uncle Chet (Chet Roble, a regular on the Studs Terkel program *Studs' Place*) as they told stories, played games, and sang songs. By the following year, the title of the show was changed to *Mary Hartline's Party*, airing at 5:30 P.M.

The enormous popularity of *Super Circus* didn't go unnoticed by the East Coast ABC honchos, who decided to move the show to New York. The last Chicago-based installment of *Super Circus* was broadcast on December 28, 1955. Mary was the only Chicago cast member asked to remain with the show; she declined, however, sticking loyally by the original cast mates.

The revamped New York version of *Super Circus* featured Jerry Colonna as ringmaster with baton-twirling Sandy Wirth as the Mary Hartline prototype. It simply didn't work. The home audience, confused and disappointed by the inexplicable change in casting, tuned out in droves, and the ratings plummeted. *Super Circus* went off the air on June 3, 1956. Within a span of six months, the network had succeeded in killing off one of its most lucrative properties.

Mary Hartline was still a major television personality in Chicago, and in 1957 she returned in *Princess Mary's Castle*. On this local half-hour program, which aired weekdays at 9:30 A.M. on Channel 7, Mary played a princess in a make-believe kingdom. Magician Don Alan was seen as court magician Sir Dono, the only other "real" person on the show.

The rest of the cast consisted of puppets created and manipulated by Bruce Newton, who had occasionally done some puppet work for *Super Circus*, and voiced by Ronny Born. There was a golden bird named Golden Bird; Kaw Crow, who collected mirrors and trinkets; his distant cousin Cuz Crow, who gave up flying; Mr. Tree; Idono, an absentminded duck; Wishing Well, a talking well; Hanky Panky, a dancing handkerchief that lived in a bottle; and Lamb, whose vocabulary was limited to one word: "Mmmmmaaa-a-a." Sir Day and Sir Night were two talking wall plaques that reported the good (and not-so-good) behavior of children. Windy Widget, a 6,000-year-old master inventor descended from a leprechaun, had a nose that grew whenever he told tall tales. To achieve this special effect, Bruce Newton gave the puppet a balloon nose that could be inflated at appropriate moments. (For more on Newton, see Chapters 6 and 15.)

Princess Mary's Castle was a morning favorite that might have enjoyed a healthy run. By 1958, however, even the energetic Hartline was running out of steam. She says, "I didn't have a real vacation for

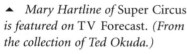

▲ *Princess Mary graces
the cover of the* Chicago
Daily Tribune TV Week.
*(From the collection of Ted
Okuda.)*

▲ *Mary Hartline of* Super Circus
is featured on TV Forecast. *(From
the collection of Ted Okuda.)*

about five years, so I needed a break. I just intended to take a little time off. But what happened was I went on vacation and never returned."

It was true love that brought the curtain down on Hartline's professional career. During a trip to the East Coast, Mary met Woolworth Donahue, an heir to the F.W. Woolworth fortune. The couple married in 1962, and Hartline never regretted her decision to leave show business.

Today, Mary Hartline is amazed by the many fans who still remember her and how well her memorabilia sells on the collector's market. Episodes of *Super Circus* are available on home video, and kinescopes (filmed versions of live broadcasts) are still being shown in countries as far away as South America.

Throughout the ups and downs of her personal and professional life, Mary has remained steadfastly optimistic: "I've always adhered to the philosophy of life suggested to me by my mother: 'If you think good and beautiful thoughts, they will be transmitted to those around you.'"

being formed, and the cost of talent rose. If Newton was going to continue to provide a voice for the goose, the station would have to pay him more money. That was an expense WBKB had no intention of shouldering, so the station simply made Garfield a speechless puppet. As puppeteer, Newton could still bang on the stage with Garfield's beak and could ring a ship's bell, but he couldn't utter a single word as he had done previously. Newton couldn't even appear on camera, as that would have placed him in a higher talent category. So from that point on, Frazier Thomas served as the "interpreter" for the delusional goose. One of Thomas's great strengths as a kiddie show host was his ability to create the illusion that he was actually communicating with the puppet.

Shortly after the show went on the air, Newton decided to leave. "It was a money issue—I wasn't making any. I got an offer from Sterling [Red] Quinlan, who was then the station program director, to join his staff. When I told Frazier, he was beside himself: 'Why are you leaving me short? Who am I going to get to manipulate Garfield Goose?' I said, 'Frazier, call the Chicago Academy of Fine Arts over on Michigan Avenue and talk with [the owner and president] Ruth Van Sickle Ford.' He called Ruth and told her the kind of person he was looking for. She said, 'Just a minute,' and looked out in the bullpen where all the new students were coming in, and said, 'Roy Brown! How'd you like to be on television?' So Roy went over to talk to Frazier and he was hired."

Frazier never forgave me for leaving the show. And for all those years, he never acknowledged my part in the creation of Garfield Goose. Later on, when they manufactured and sold a cheap cloth version of the Garfield puppet, I threatened legal action, so they pulled it off the market. I guess that proves I had some claim to Garfield, but Frazier still shut me out, right up to the day he died.
    —Bruce Newton

Frazier was quite mad at Bruce. And for his own reasons, he never gave Bruce any credit for his role.
    —Sterling Quinlan to *Chicago Tribune*
    columnist Eric Zorn

Roy Thomas Brown was a 20-year-old art student when Thomas hired him. Over the next four decades, Brown's puppet creations delighted generations of Chicago-area children. For *Garfield Goose*, Brown created the "friends." Romberg Rabbit was an unemployed magician's assistant who frequently served as go-between for the volatile goose and his put-upon prime minister. The cast also included deerstalker-hatted Beauregard Burnside III, the world's sleepiest bloodhound; cute little MacIntosh Mouse; and Christmas Goose, the king's preppy nephew. The character of Mama Goose—a seasonal visitor from Goosejaw, Saskatchewan—was simply the Garfield Goose puppet with a wig, shawl, and wire-rimmed glasses. Brown also served as puppeteer and brought a remarkable array of body language to all the characters.

In an interview with Chicago journalist Jim Mueller, Roy Brown recalled:

> With Beauregard Burnside III, Frazier said, "Wouldn't it be nice to have a secret service agent and make him a bloodhound who can't stay awake?" I sculpted Beau in clay first, then molded him in solastic [moldable plastic]. Romberg Rabbit [named after WGN staffer Don Romberg] was created earlier for a kids' show called *Quiet Riot* starring Buddy Black. Frazier liked the character so much, we added him to *Garfield Goose*.
>
> Frazier was a perfectionist who insisted on a tightly scripted show. We didn't have much ad-libbing like you saw on *Bozo*. But I did have freedom to be creative with the characters. I could even make Garfield smile. When I pulled my thumb back three-quarters of an inch or so it would put just the right wrinkle in his cloth, and he'd smile.

After a move to WBBM in 1953 and back to WBKB in 1954, *Garfield Goose and Friend* wound up on WGN in 1955, where it stayed for the next 21 years (the title was eventually changed to *Garfield Goose and Friends*).

The show opened with a trumpet blare, segueing into the Ethel Smith organ tune "Monkey on a String." (Historian Rick Goldschmidt recently traced the Ethel Smith album the tune comes from: *Bright and*

▲ *A postcard sent out to fans of* Garfield Goose and Friends *shows (left to right) Romberg Rabbit, Beauregard Burnside III, Garfield Goose (wearing a different crown), MacIntosh Mouse, Frazier Thomas, and Chris (Christmas) Goose. (Courtesy of the Mark Yurkiw collection.)*

Breezy.) As the music played, an animated banner bearing Garfield's likeness would give way to Roy Brown's artwork of a royal castle. Then fade to Frazier standing in front of a brick castle wall with an opening that served as the puppet stage.

The first time I met Frazier Thomas was back in 1960. For some reason, I was in the Tribune Tower, where WGN had its studio at that time. I saw "Frazier Thomas and Garfield Goose" on the door, so I decided to walk in and introduce myself. Frazier, who didn't know me from Adam, was sitting at the main desk, like a receptionist. When I introduced myself as a puppeteer, he laughed for a bit, then called out to Roy Brown, who was in another room. He said, "Hey, Roy, come out here—this guy's a puppeteer! You know, you're the first puppeteer we've ever met." Then he took

a magnifying glass and checked me over, and said, in a condescending tone, "God, you look as normal as we do. Well, we've finally met a puppeteer! Isn't that something!" I kept thinking "This is weird!"
—Jack Mulqueen

During the late '60s and early '70s, I attended Lane Technical High School on Addison Street, which is located across the way from WGN's studio on Bradley Place. On occasion, I'd see Frazier Thomas on the Addison Street bus, which always mystified me. I watched his show for years and I figured he rode to work in a limousine that was adorned with Garfield Goose banners and similar paraphernalia. But no, he just sat there, always in the seat immediately behind the driver, like a work-a-day Joe commuting to his job.
—Ted Okuda

It was at WGN that the show solidified what would become its trademark segments. The Little Theater Screen (originally conceived by Bruce Newton), on which the cartoons were supposedly projected, had been part of the program since its earliest days and was still a fixture. Cartoons like *Clutch Cargo, The Mighty Hercules,* and *Bucky and Pepito* were standard bill of fare. But one of the most intriguing series featured on the show was a serialized adventure called *Journey to the Beginning of Time.*

Journey to the Beginning of Time is the Americanized version of *Cesta do praveku* ("Voyage to Prehistory"), a 1955 feature-length movie directed by Czechoslovakian filmmaker Karel Zeman. A former poster designer, Zeman made movies that skillfully combined live action, animation, puppetry, and models. His other films include *Vynalez zkazy* (1958; "An Invention of Destruction"), released in the United States in 1961 as *The Fabulous World of Jules Verne,* and *Baron Prasil* (1961; *The Fabulous Baron Munchausen,* 1964).

Cesta do praveku tells the story of four boys who go boating down a mysterious river and wind up traveling back in time, encountering a variety of prehistoric creatures along the way. In the late 1950s, William Cayton, an American producer, secured the U.S. distribution rights to the film and added new opening scenes involving the American

sea voyage on a two-masted 85-foot schooner, he filmed their experiences, as he did when they visited England. Thomas turned this footage into entertaining specials for WGN: *Sailing the Seas of Columbus* and *The Legend of Arthur the Phantom King*. Both were later serialized on *Garfield Goose*.

Thomas described these specials to Ed Schwartz:

> [The specials] were a labor of love with me. I had a wonderful time doing it. It took me six months to research [*The Legend of Arthur the Phantom King*] and I spent a month filming it. I worked another six months before I ever put it on tape. I spent my own money; it didn't cost the station a thing. I thought it was the kind of thing that youngsters really should see. That was the reason I did it.
>
> But I must tell you that the station never looked upon it as a particularly interesting thing. They looked at it and said, "Well, let him run that because he liked to do it."

It was an event when you went anywhere with Frazier because he was so recognized. He was always charming—every minute! And it was not a fake.

—WGN music director Bob Trendler

There was a Greek restaurateur who used to appear frequently on WGN's weather reports because he claimed he had the ability to talk to fish, and they would tell him what the weather would be. Somehow, he impressed the station enough to put him on the air and let him quote his predictions. Every time he'd run into Frazier, he would invite Frazier and his family to the Greek restaurant. After repeated invitations, Frazier weakened and drove to the restaurant one Sunday afternoon. When he got there, he saw a huge sign in front of the place: "FRAZIER THOMAS APPEARING HERE TODAY." Inside, Frazier and his family were surrounded by fans. Frazier was as obliging as he could be, as he ate his meal and signed autographs. When he was finished, the owner thanked him for stopping by — and presented him a bill for the meals!

—Jack Mulqueen

When Ned Locke—Ringmaster Ned on *Bozo's Circus*—retired in 1976, WGN decided to add Frazier Thomas to the circus roster. Frazier appeared on Locke's final *Bozo* show (taped July 9, 1976; broadcast July 23, 1976) to explain to TV viewers that Garfield Goose had purchased the circus from Ringmaster Ned and then appointed Frazier as the new circus manager.

Thomas took over as the full-time host of *Bozo's Circus* on Tuesday, July 27, 1976. *Garfield Goose and Friends* continued as a separate program through September 10, 1976, at which time the show ended its astounding 24-year Chicago-area run.

Although the change was an economically logical one for WGN, it shattered the genteel universe that Thomas had so carefully crafted. Amidst the freewheeling antics of clowns Bozo (Bob Bell), Cooky (Roy Brown), and Wizzo (Marshall Brodien), Thomas often appeared to be at a loss to deal with his new environment. *Bozo* producer Al Hall remembers, "When Frazier was doing Garfield Goose, he was in charge, he ran the show. And he was very concerned when he came to *Bozo* because of all the ad-lib, impromptu stuff we did. That was not the way he was accustomed to working."

In the summer of 1980, the title was changed to *The Bozo Show*. Beginning January 26, 1981, the format was expanded to 90 minutes, it went from being broadcast live to being taped in advance, and Garfield Goose was replaced by Cuddley Dudley, previously a fixture on *Ray Rayner and His Friends*. (Rayner had just retired.) As a result, Frazier Thomas served only as a host and straight man to the clowns. There were times during his *Bozo* stint that Thomas seemed clearly perplexed and more than a bit agitated—which is understandable, considering that he was frequently the target of his cast mates' practical jokes. Bob Bell loved to relate a story about a time when he and the other clowns got together and decided to perform a completely different comedy sketch, which sent the always-prepared Frazier into a panic.

Frazier and I were good friends. Sometimes when Roy Brown was sick or needed to take days off, I'd work the puppets on Garfield Goose. When they added Frazier to the Bozo *cast, I thought it was a big mistake. He*

▲ *Cooky and Bozo welcomed Garfield Goose and Frazier Thomas to the cast of* Bozo's Circus *in 1976. (Courtesy of the Mark Yurkiw collection.)*

already had a great show, so why tamper with it? But WGN *wanted to make the change. Frazier was simply miscast.*
      — *Bozo's Circus* writer-performer-producer
      Don Sandburg

Frazier was used to adhering to a script so closely, and we were ad-libbing completely. Frazier would get so frustrated because he had been accustomed all these years to a very formal script.
      —Bob Bell in a WGN interview

Frazier was an interesting person. He was probably a little more straight-laced than you would suspect. And he was a control freak.
      —Al Hall

(For more on *Bozo's Circus*, see Chapter 12.)

On Monday morning, April 1, 1985, Frazier Thomas suffered a cerebral hemorrhage at the WGN studio. A maintenance employee found him collapsed in the hallway, and he was rushed to the hospital. As it was only a few hours before a *Bozo Show* taping, cast member Pat Hurley was recruited to fill in for him. Thomas passed away two days later, on April 3.

After Frazier's death, WGN had six weeks of pretaped *Bozo* programs to air, followed by a summer of reruns. Before the show, a graphic would be flashed on the screen as a staff announcer somberly intoned, "The following program was prerecorded." (Frazier's pretaped introductions for the *Transformers* cartoons would air as late as September 1985.)

Soon after his passing, WGN broadcast *Frazier Thomas: A Family Classic,* an affectionate tribute written and hosted by newscaster Steve Sanders. On the show, Roy Brown remarked, "I think [*Garfield Goose*] was successful because it was good, clean, wholesome entertainment. The whole family could enjoy it and Frazier never talked down to children. He respected children and I know that came across on television."

In Thomas's honor, the 2500 block of West Bradley Place—the address of WGN-TV—was renamed Frazier Thomas Place.

At the time of his death, Thomas had written his autobiography and nine children's books centering around a new character, Gulliver Goose, with such titles as "Gulliver Goose and the Lost Gold Mine" and "Gulliver Goose and the Rocket to the Moon." (As of April 2004, none of these manuscripts had been published.)

Frazier Thomas's legacy stands as a shining example of what quality family programming should be but seldom is: edifying, tasteful, fun, and, above all, brimming with charm.

on the air the following month. The producer was Fred Silverman, who would later become president of the ABC and NBC networks. Rayner told Ed Schwartz:

> Fred was then producing *Breakfast with Bugs Bunny*—the morning spot I eventually took over—and *Family Classics*. WGN had just bought a brand new package of Dick Tracy cartoons. In those days, when you got a children's television show, usually they said, "You've got these cartoons . . . now it's up to you to come up with ideas and fill up the rest of the time. Just keep talking and when you run out of words, put a cartoon on."
>
> In working with Fred, I started to get nervous because neither he nor I could jell on a format. I was about a week away from going on the air in a brand new show with a lot of publicity and promotion, and we had a creative block. So I went to the WGN program director and said, "I hate to say this, but Fred and I aren't jelling on production ideas." He said, "Don't worry about it. I'll get you somebody else," and he got me a fine producer named Hal Stein. Then he added, and I'll never forget these words, "But Ray, watch that kid. I think he's gonna do something in this business."
>
> Even though Fred and I only worked together about three or four days, I didn't think he was a producer of any great stature. That isn't his forte. But it's obvious he's strong on knowing how to program against competition. *The Dick Tracy Show* had a strange time slot—6:30 P.M.—when it debuted. When I was introduced to Fred, he immediately said, "Do you know who your competition is? Steve Allen!" He always thought about who was on the air against you, and how to compete against it.

The Dick Tracy Show debuted on September 11, 1961, featuring Rayner as Sgt. Henry Pettibone, who, in his Crime Stopper Cruiser vehicle, introduced Dick Tracy cartoons and handled radio communications from various sectors of law enforcement. Each half-hour show featured two Dick Tracy cartoons and one Q.T. Hush cartoon. (Hush, who was always seen wearing a Sherlock Holmes deerstalker cap, was another animated crime fighter.)

The Dick Tracy cartoons were produced by United Productions of America (UPA), an animation studio that enjoyed great acclaim for its minimalist style and characters such as Mr. Magoo and Gerald McBoing Boing. Veteran character actor Everett Sloane provided the voice for Dick Tracy in these five-minute made-for-TV cartoons. Strangely, the Tracy character barely appeared in the cartoons that bore his name. Instead, the World's Greatest Crime Stopper became, in these efforts, the World's Laziest Law Enforcer.

After a speeding squad car opening, each cartoon began with Tracy receiving an urgent call from headquarters. "I'll get on it right away, Chief," he'd intone, then promptly pass the assignment off to one of his assistants. While villains like Flat Top and Pruneface came right out of the pages of the Dick Tracy comic strips, his assistants were strictly UPA creations. Thus Tracy would call upon Heap O'Calorie (voiced by Johnny Coons) or Hemlock Holmes (voiced by Jerry Hauser) and the Retouchables, Holmes's Keystone Kops-like police squad.

These characters were harmless enough, but two of Tracy's assistants relied heavily on racial stereotypes: Japanese detective Joe Jitsu (voiced by Benny Rubin) and Mexican sleuth Go Go Gomez (voiced

◀ *Ray Rayner's coveralls on display at Chicago's Museum of Broadcast Communications. (Courtesy of David Maska.)*

by Mel Blanc, who did nearly all the classic Warner Brothers characters). At the time, they didn't cause a stir, but seen today, they're pretty cringe-inducing, with lines like "Hold everything, *preeze*! This is
porice!" and "*Ay, chihuahua!* Señor Tracee eez en *trooble*!" sounding
especially horrific. (When these cartoons were resurrected for the
home video and cable TV markets in 1990 to capitalize on Warren
Beatty's *Dick Tracy* movie, there was such a public outcry that the
series was quickly withdrawn from distribution.)

In the 1960s, however, there was no apparent objection over this
material, and *The Dick Tracy Show* became a popular favorite. Sgt.
Pettibone was assisted by Tracer, a dog puppet (designed and built by
Roy Brown) always seen in a basket on Pettibone's desk. Initially,
Tracer was a nameless, abandoned puppy found by Pettibone. After the
show had been on the air three weeks, WGN ran a "name the dog" contest that resulted in a staggering 30,000 entries received by the station.
The judges decided on Tracer as the winning name. Although several
dozen entrants suggested the name, the prize—a real puppy—was
awarded to the young boy who sent in the first letter suggesting Tracer,
and he even appeared on the show to accept his prize.

Impressionist Ron MacAdam provided the voice for Tracer and also
worked the puppet from underneath the desk. Rayner once remarked
to Ed Schwartz, "Ron had never worked with puppets before, and he
turned out to be one of the best puppeteers you could find. He just
had a feeling for it. He even gave Tracer different 'moods.'"

MacAdam also did all the off-camera voices (including Dick Tracy
in scenes specially made for syndication as a tie-in for local hosts) and
appeared on camera in various roles (such as Scoop Wilson, reporter
for the Exaggerated Press). By the time the show ended its run in 1966,
MacAdam had played an estimated total of 58 characters.

The Dick Tracy Show was originally seen each weekday at 6:30 P.M.
It was a ratings hit, prompting WGN to move it to a 4:30 P.M. time slot,
where audience numbers increased even further. Shortly after New
Year's 1962, the program offered viewers a chance to become members
of Dick Tracy's Crime Stopper Club by sending away for an Official
Crime Stopper Kit, which contained a membership card and oath, a
badge, and—perhaps most important of all—a secret code decoder.

(The decoder allowed users to translate secret messages relayed by Sgt. Pettibone.) This promotion turned out to be too successful: Within a short span of time, there were more than 130,000 Crime Stopper Club members, making the promised monthly newsletter too cost-prohibitive for WGN. At this point, the station curtailed its membership promotion.

On Monday, November 6, 1961, about two months after he began *The Dick Tracy Show*, Rayner joined the cast of *Bozo's Circus*. He appeared as Oliver O. Oliver, a clown from Puff Bluff, Kentucky, who would serve as perennial fall guy for Bozo's schemes and practical jokes. (For more on Rayner's involvement with *Bozo's Circus*, see Chapter 12.)

In addition to his *Dick Tracy Show* and *Bozo's Circus* duties, Rayner took over the hosting chores of *Breakfast with Bugs Bunny* in 1962, replacing Dick Coughlan. When the show was rechristened *Ray Rayner and His Friends* in 1964, it took on a formless, at times surreal format: a parade of cartoons interspersed by some indulgent segments.

Rayner, wearing the note-riddled jumpsuit that became his trademark, would often open the show with a song—warbling in his self-proclaimed "whiskey baritone"—accompanied by musical director Harold Turner (and later, Don Orlando). It could be a novelty tune ("How Much Is That Doggie in the Window?"), something relevant to the season ("Let It Snow" was a popular choice during the winter months), or a surprisingly urbane selection (Rayner may be the only kiddie show host who ever sang "My Funny Valentine" on his program). As Rayner was vocalizing, director Bill Hartmann had the cameras cut to various areas of the set, with close-ups of things like a framed picture, a door, a wall clock . . . nothing that was relevant to the lyrics, or particularly interesting, either.

Then Ray would introduce a classic Warner Brothers cartoon, usually one starring Bugs Bunny. At the time, WGN's library consisted of the pre-1948 Warners cartoons,[2] many of them from the World War II era. In the early days of the show, these cartoons were aired uncut, even though they were rife with sexual innuendos, racial stereotyping, and violent gags involving handguns and sledgehammers. It wasn't until the program's final years that these cartoons were edited (several were shredded to ribbons) or shelved entirely.

What followed afterward was anybody's guess, though there were a stock number of regular features that could be trotted out. Sometimes it would be a comedy bit, with Ray playing newscaster Walter Winkley of PBS (Pretend Broadcasting System).[3] Sometimes he'd simply walk over to a closet, grab a band uniform and a baton, announce "Let's march!", then proceed to do so for the next couple minutes.

Other times he'd feed a live duck he called Chelveston, named after the English air base where Rayner served during World War II. (*Remember? By George, now you've got it!*) Chelveston, who replaced Havelock, came to the show courtesy of the Animal Kingdom pet shop on Milwaukee Avenue in Chicago. Rayner explained to Ed Schwartz:

▶ *A postcard sent out to fans of* Ray Rayner and His Friends (The Ray Rayner Show) *shows Rayner holding Chelveston the duck. (Courtesy of the Mark Yurkiw collection.)*

Chelveston lived at the Animal Kingdom and got a free ride to the station every weekday. It was a strange arrangement, though, because after the pet shop closed in the early evening, they would bring Chelveston over to WGN at night. He'd stay in the hall all night long and then go on the air with me at 7 A.M. One problem was that everybody walking down the hall at night—engineers, news writers—would give him a little something to eat. Then he'd come on my show, and he wouldn't be hungry. When I'd try to feed him lettuce or duck pellets, he'd walk away because he was too full.

Chelveston was strange around me. I could never get him to be as close to me as he was with every stagehand, every cameraman, and every guest who walked into the studio. He'd go right over to them. But with me, he had to be really hungry.

Chelveston would frequently snap at Rayner's heels, to the delight of viewers at home and the studio crew. "He used to chase me all around the studio, nipping at my ankles. I used to put in tin man leggings so he'd bang away at the leggings. Then he'd calm down." (The ankle nipping became such an anticipated bit that cereal was occasionally put in the cuffs of Rayner's trousers to encourage the duck to attack.) The segment usually concluded with Ray giving Chelveston a bath by placing him in an on-set bathtub.

One regular feature that was a surefire hit with young viewers was the "Do It Yourself" segment. As versatile as he was, Rayner had zero ability when it came to arts-and-crafts projects. He was all thumbs when handling scissors, and more glue wound up on his hands than on the item he was constructing. Sometimes he would misread the printed instructions and wind up skipping a crucial step toward completion. Thus making a toothbrush holder or pincushion from simple household objects became, in Rayner's hands, a task tantamount to detonating a nuclear bomb.

Rayner would then hold up his finished work—which bore no resemblance to the beautifully constructed sample items created by Diane Flanders of the WGN art department—and, with a self-deprecating chuckle, announce, "You can do it yourself!" The beauty of all

produced 260 episodes of *Space Angel*. With that much footage available, *Rocket to Adventure* was able to make the series a main focal point of the show. (*Gigantor* and *Tobor the 8th Man* were dropped at one point because of complaints about violent content.)

With its science fiction–themed cartoons and a periodic "space walk" outside the ship by Rayner, *Rocket to Adventure* enjoyed a two-season run, leaving the air in 1968. Not that Rayner had to worry about keeping busy. He still had *Ray Rayner and His Friends* in the morning and *Bozo's Circus* at noon.

From 1968 to 1969, Rayner was the first "talking" Ronald McDonald on television. Up until that time, Ronald had been a mute clown in the McDonald's commercials. Rayner was selected by the hamburger firm to appear as Ronald and deliver dialogue, which he did, using his Oliver O. Oliver voice. Over a two-year period, Ray was seen and heard in 12 to 15 McDonald's commercials, all of which were shot on weekends in San Diego.

In 1971 Rayner left *Bozo's Circus*, although he would continue to make occasional appearances on the show, both as himself and as Oliver O. Oliver. He now had the time to appear on the station's lottery broadcasts and the remotes from the annual Chicago Auto Show. In 1976 he hosted a Wednesday night movie showcase sponsored by Prince Spaghetti ("Wednesday is Prince Spaghetti night!").

Throughout his years at WGN, Rayner appeared in 30 to 40 local theatrical productions. He performed in several plays at the Candlelight Theater in Summit, Illinois; starred in a production of *Plaza Suite* with Polly Bergen at the Drury Lane South; and, in 1979, opened the Drury Lane East at McCormick Place in *40 Carats* with Ginger Rogers. It made for a grueling work schedule, but Rayner loved every minute of it.

In early 1979, Rayner renewed his WGN contract for another two years. However, while driving to his Northbrook home in the middle of a particularly nasty winter snowstorm, he made the decision to leave Chicago when his contract expired.

December 18, 1980, marked the final live broadcast of *Ray Rayner and His Friends*. Pretaped shows aired for the next few weeks. A pretaped farewell program was scheduled for January 30, 1981, but when

▲ *Bill Jackson (*The B.J. and Dirty Dragon Show*), Ray Rayner, and Beverly Marston Braun (*Romper Room*) signing autographs at Chicago's Museum of Broadcast Communications on April 21, 2001. (Courtesy of David Maska.)*

WGN decided to end the show's run a week earlier than planned, it ran on January 23 instead, with all references to January 30 bleeped out.

By the time his farewell show aired, Rayner had moved from Chicago to Albuquerque, New Mexico. "I felt I couldn't stand another Chicago winter," Rayner told Deborah Dowley Preiser. "After I got here, I regretted leaving when I did. I should have stayed another ten years. It was a great job."

If Rayner took his show for granted, then so did his audience. His departure from the Chicago television scene is a prime example of not appreciating what you have until it's gone. For many Chicago-area kids, it was "Ray in the morning," then off to school, only to see him again at lunchtime and in the afternoon. He was a reassuring, constant figure during the formative years of so many viewers, an indelible part of their childhood. To say he was missed is an understatement.

Ray Rayner was perhaps the most unlikely idol in the history of Chicago television. Yet he won us over by simply being himself. He was Everyman with the soul of Everychild.

1. Mark Yurkiw notes that there were times during the show's 17 years when it ran only an hour or 75 minutes.

2. In the mid- to late 1960s, WGN acquired another 100 Warner Brothers cartoons, from the 1948–60 period. In the mid-1970s, the station picked up an additional 156 Porky Pig cartoons, some colorized.

3. Rayner's PBS predated today's Public Broadcasting System, which was then called NET (National Educational Television). NET became PBS in the early 1970s.

A Trunk Full of Memories

John Conrad and Elmer the Elephant

Kids love elephants and our show was pure slapstick. So what's not to like?
— John Conrad

One of the most fondly remembered Chicago kid programs featured a mischievous elephant and his exasperated caretaker. *Elmer the Elephant*, the "Peck's Bad Boy of Television," had no educational agenda, no life lessons to impart, no messages to preach. It was just a half hour of pure hokum, none of it subtle, but irresistibly funny nevertheless. This was good, old-fashioned, knockabout slapstick, delivered with gusto by the energetic host, John Conrad. Conrad's only goal was to entertain his audience, which he did expertly throughout his show business career.

Born and reared in Blue Island, Illinois, John Conrad began his professional career as a page at WNBQ, Chicago's NBC affiliate. Conrad recalls:

> I conducted studio tours for about two years. Then I auditioned as an announcer for a show called *The Morris B. Sachs Amateur Hour.* I did well and went on to WIND radio, where I was on a show with Charlie Grimm, the former manager of the Chicago Cubs. Charlie would do the Game of the Day, where he'd re-create baseball games off the Teletype. He'd have a bat hanging from the ceiling; when somebody got a hit, he'd re-create the sound by hitting the bat with a smaller bat. He'd also have a baseball glove on his desk; when there was a "ball," he'd slam a baseball into the glove. I did the commercials for Wrigley Gum.
>
> Jules Herbuveaux was the vice president and general manager of WNBQ. I got to know him, and he liked my work. One day he had me audition for some folks from El Paso, Texas. Now, by this time, I was making $200 a week, which was pretty good money in those days, especially for a single guy. I mean, a married guy with a family rarely made that kind of money. But I wound up accepting an offer at KTSM in El Paso for $115 a month, because Jules said, "You need the experience, and they'll teach you everything you need to know." So I went down there, and everything worked out fine. In fact, that's where I met my wife.
>
> Then I went into the navy for four years. After I got out, Bill Kephardt, the chief announcer at WNBQ, called me and said, "John, you can come back to work for us, no strings attached." I went back to work for the station and wound up staying there 23 years.

Conrad began his television career reading the funny papers on the air on a Sunday morning show called *Sunday Funnies.* He also did commercials for RCA Victor on *Kukla, Fran & Ollie* and hosted a game show, *Take a Dare.* His assistants on *Take a Dare* were Hugh Downs (who was later seen on *The Today Show, The Jack Paar Show, Concentration,* and *20/20*) and comedian Cliff Norton.

bubble of pomposity. He always tried to lecture or get the best of Elmer, but the pachyderm would prevail in the end, as Conrad wound up on the receiving end of seltzer water, pies, or bags of flour.

Conrad recalls:

> I wrote a major portion of the show, and I got help from a staff writer named Bob Carmen. Bill Daily, who later appeared on *I Dream of Jeannie* and *The Bob Newhart Show*, was our floor director, and we had some fantastic stagehands.
>
> I'm a big fan of Laurel & Hardy, and we patterned the show after their style of comedy. For every routine we did, I played the Oliver Hardy part, the guy who thought he knew it all. We figured the kids could identify with Elmer, since they always felt like they were being dominated by an authority figure. So when Elmer got the best of me, it was like a victory for the kids.

The show featured cartoons and Little Rascals comedy shorts, but viewers really tuned in to see the crazy antics of Conrad and Elmer. The heavy emphasis on sight gags and physical humor made it necessary to have multiple costumes and puppets. Conrad remembers:

> Elmer always used to get me with a bag of flour or a pie made out of shaving cream. I had four circus uniforms, and they were always being changed. After every show, I had to go to my dressing room, which was down the hall from the studio. So I'd be coming down the hallway and all these business people would be shocked to see me in a circus uniform covered with flour and shaving cream. They didn't know what to think.
>
> We used to have several Elmer heads because sometimes the one we were using started to get some wear and had to be refurbished. We would worry about using a "fresh" head because we thought viewers might notice the difference, but no one ever did.
>
> We even tried to work in another puppet, a female elephant named Elmira, but it didn't pan out. The idea faded because she just didn't have the appeal of Elmer, so the character was dropped.

◀ *John Conrad of* Elmer the Elephant *in "civilian" apparel. (Courtesy of John Conrad.)*

In 1954 *Elmer the Elephant* won the *TV Guide* Chicago Award for Best Children's Show. The show was so popular that the network expanded its running time to help the ratings of another program. Conrad explains, "There was a show that followed us at 5:30 p.m. NBC didn't like the ratings it was getting so they said, 'Okay, John, we're going to run *Elmer* from 5 to 5:35, so you'll bleed into the next show and help them along.' We did and the strategy worked."

Although the show still had a huge following, *Elmer the Elephant* was canceled in 1956. Conrad remembers, "NBC in New York decided to go to adult programming during my time slot, so they dumped us. After they did, they could never find a successful replacement. The ratings for that time period just kept sinking lower and lower. So six years later, they brought us back."

Elmer returned in 1962 with the same show, same formula. "It was identical to what we had been doing before," says Conrad. "If you've got a winning formula, why mess with it?"

pets. But I didn't want her in traditional clown makeup. I thought, 'Why hide a pretty face?'"

Marquee and Stage Door came to a halt when Jack was honorably discharged from the army. He enrolled in college on the G.I. Bill and entertained thoughts of pursuing a career as a teacher . . . until he discovered the campus radio station as well as a nearby television station. In addition to hosting a college radio program, Jack conceived a one-hour TV special titled *The Missing Circus Whistle*, which showcased— what else?—his puppets. "On that show, we had Audrey McMillen appear as a pixie clown I called 'Pandora' . . . again, a clown without the traditional makeup."

Going home for Easter vacation, Jack found himself one evening at the Holiday Ballroom, a dance hall on Chicago's South Side. There he asked a pretty young lady named Elaine Pazak for a dance. "I told her I was a puppeteer and she asked, 'Do you make money doing that?' Unfortunately, the answer was no. Nevertheless, when I met her again a month later, I knew I was in love with her. To make a long story short, we were married a year later."

▶ *Del Bremicker and Audree McMillan support fellow college student and puppeteer Jack Mulqueen on* The Missing Circus Whistle *TV special,* WTHI-TV, *Terre Haute, Indiana (1954). (From the Mulqueen archives.)*

After less than two years of college, Mulqueen set out to pursue a career as a professional puppeteer, only to discover that the Chicago television market wasn't clamoring for one. He remembers:

I spent about a year doing odd jobs, from setting up window displays to selling sportswear. I went to work for a film company that made trailers [coming attractions] and publicity photos for movie theaters. Their production quota was 250 photos a day, but no matter how hard I tried, I could only print 150. After three weeks, I was handed my check and my notice. It was then that I decided if I couldn't find any immediate prospects I should create one.

I wound up going to Channel 11 (the independent WTTW, which later became Chicago's PBS affiliate) and told them I was working for the Chicago Park District and asked if they would like to have an experienced puppeteer put on a weekly program sponsored by the District. They quickly agreed to my proposal. Then I went to the Park District and told them I had a show lined up and asked if they would like to sponsor it. They loved the idea, and only a few weeks after I married Elaine, I was not only the very first puppeteer hired by the Park District, but I also had a television segment every Monday at 5 P.M.

Mulqueen and his puppets appeared Mondays on Channel 11's *The Totem Club,* a children's variety show. "Joe Kelly was the host; he had formerly been the host of popular shows like *Quiz Kids* and *National Barn Dance.* He helped me out by hiring me to work with him at school shows throughout the year. He was the first real talent I had the chance to work with, and his words of encouragement went a long way in my determination to get my own show."

During his five-year stint with the Chicago Park District, Jack honed his skills as a puppeteer and self-promoter. He staged puppet shows and taught children how to make their own puppets. He sold the Borden Dairy Company on the idea of "Elsie the Cow's Puppet Carnival," touring food stores and shopping centers.

When only 15 kids turned out for his first shopping center appearance, Mulqueen began to realize the importance of publicity. He dis-

▲ *Early in their television careers, Elaine Mulqueen (as Pandora) and Jack Mulqueen (with his puppets) played parking lots and super markets (1962). (From the Mulqueen archives.)*

tributed handbills, glad-handed merchants, and didn't let a single publicity angle slip by. When the police halted a performance because someone had neglected to obtain a proper permit, Jack contacted a local newspaper, resulting in a "COPS RAID KIDDIE SHOW" article. In a canny effort to increase revenue, Mulqueen mounted five duplicate versions of his puppet show, enabling him to saturate the Chicagoland area.

All along, Mulqueen's shows featured a pixie clown named Pandora, who served as a combination cheerleader–comic foil for Jack's puppets. Numerous young ladies were hired to play the role. They came and went, for various reasons; one was fired because Jack caught her shoplifting during a food store appearance.

Eventually, and fortuitously, Elaine Mulqueen was recruited to become a Pandora. Jack recalls, "When you work for the Park District, you have certain 'obligations.' Every year, a particular Chicago alderman would throw a big Christmas party at the Century Theater. It was for the kids in the neighborhood, and there would be movies and some stage acts. And every year the Park District would inform me that 'You *will* appear at the Century.' Well, one year I completely ignored the edict, and they didn't come to me until a week or two before the annual party. I said I already had other commitments, but they firmly told me, 'No excuses!'"

Elaine adds, "Jack was in a spot, so I said, 'Let me fill in for you. After all, they're still going to get a Mulqueen.' But I didn't think of it as anything permanent; he had other Pandoras."

"It turned out that Elaine was very well received," Jack continues. "In fact, they even paid her for her appearance . . . and they *never* paid me. I had a young lady who I trained to be a puppeteer, but she didn't have anyone to go on stage with her, so I couldn't book her for any appearances. Howard Schultz, an agent we knew, sent Elaine out on a couple more appearances with this gal, and word came back that Elaine got a better reception than any other act Howard booked during this period. Howard said to me, 'I don't know what you need those other girls for.' He was right. I didn't want to push Elaine into anything, but it turned out she came to the rescue and stayed."

Elaine didn't have any acting ambitions or experience, but her vivacious personality and her obvious love of children registered strongly with her audience. She reflects, "The fact that I'd be around kids was the reason I agreed to join the act. If it were strictly for an adult audience, I would have told Jack to find someone else. I've never felt comfortable performing in front of adults, but in front of kids, that's something else. I feel totally at ease with them because they're completely honest with you. If they're having a good time, their appreciation is immediate and genuine; there's nothing false about their response. It's funny, but I was always more comfortable in front of thousands of children than I was in front of a dozen adults. I learned to block the adults out of my mind and just concentrate on the kids. As long as I did that, I was just fine."

By the summer of 1960, "Elsie the Cow's Puppet Carnival" was completely booked, and the Mulqueens were holding talks with the Coca-Cola Bottling Company, which was interested in sponsoring similar shows. One sour note during this period, however, was WTTW dropping Jack from its roster.

In 1962 Jack and Elaine got their first big TV break on WGN's *Bozo's Circus*, which was then the most popular kid show in Chicago. As pixie

▲ *Pandora and Mr. Hands (Elaine and Jack Mulqueen) pose to promote their new show on WGN,* The Mulqueens. *(From the Mulqueen archives.)*

clown Pandora, Elaine wore a harlequin costume, while Jack served as puppeteer and frequently appeared on camera as Mr. Hands. Adorned with a fright wig, bulb nose, and rumpled hat, Mr. Hands was sort of a variation of Sid Caesar's German professor character and allowed Jack to indulge in his fondness for comic accents.

Monday through Friday they performed a one-minute Coca-Cola commercial ("Fun Time or Play Time Is a Great Time for Coke Time"). Once a week they performed a five-minute skit. "I hired a talented young man named George Bloom to write comedy material for us," Jack remembers. "His stuff was terrific, and the fact that he went on to write for Dean Martin, Bob Hope, and Milton Berle reinforces my opinion."

Jack and Elaine's segment was supposed to be called "The Mulqueens' Puppet Carnival." But when "Ringmaster Ned" Locke forgot the exact title and introduced them as simply "The Mulqueens,"

Jack liked the sound of it, enough to utilize the title later on.

After six months as glorified guest stars, Jack felt that the Mulqueens were ready for a show of their own. He recalls:

> Phil Meyer was the assistant program director at WGN. After going back and forth with him for over a year, he finally agreed to a meeting early in 1963. The first thing he asked me was, "What have you been doing lately?" I told him, "Well, I've been appearing each week on your station, on your top-rated kids' show, *Bozo's Circus.*" After weeks of discussion with Meyer and WGN's sales manager, the station informed me that if I could come up with $1,200 each week, they would give us the 9 A.M. time slot on Saturday mornings. This meant that I not only had to find sponsors who would cover the base $1,200 cost, but I also had to pay additional funds to cover our salaries, the cost of sets, scripts, and all the other production expenses. My plan was to sell three sponsors, each a third of the show, consisting of two one-minute commercials, plus a ten-second opening and closing credits. But our involvement wouldn't end there. I'd present a merchandising package to potential sponsors, outlining that Elaine and I would go to extra lengths to promote their product. We'd be willing to make personal appearances at schools, stores, and shopping centers . . . whatever it took.
>
> Bordens, Coca-Cola, and the Vienna Sausage Company were interested in signing on, but they were all taking their time in making a definite commitment. In desperation, I told each of them, separately, that I had already sold two-thirds of the show and that they had to decide quickly because I had several sponsors waiting in line. They all jumped at the chance to become the third sponsor, and were glad to get in on what seemed like an exclusive deal. My ploy worked, but I felt guilty about it for a long time afterwards.
>
> An independent producer has more on his plate than someone who's on staff. In addition to my performing duties, I would contact the transcription department for music clearance, then the art department for set design. Then there were special effects, transition slides—so the screen wouldn't go

him to wait a few more weeks until the A.C. Nielsen ratings came out and use that as a guide in making a decision, not some agency's private survey. But I knew Ed was being pressured.

When I left his office, I was as low as a man can get. I had another appointment that day, and it was at Angel Guardian Orphanage, where I did volunteer work with children. However, I really felt like heading to the nearest bar where I could figuratively and literally cry in my beer. I kept telling myself that I couldn't let those kids down, so I headed for the orphanage, praying to God all the way there.

While I was sitting there showing the children how to make puppets, a 12-year-old boy—whose name I'm sorry to say I don't remember—asked me out of the blue, "Mr. Mulqueen, how would you like to know what your television rating is?" In shock, my response was to ask him how a boy his age knew about such things. He informed me that a woman from the Nielsen bureau also worked with the orphans. When he told her he watched *The Mulqueens,* she mentioned to him that she was working on the Saturday morning ratings, and knew the results several weeks before a printed version would be distributed. Days later, Sister Angelona, the nun in charge of the orphanage, congratulated me on having a higher rating than *Shari Lewis & Lambchop,* which was a network series on NBC. It turned out that we were watched in almost 50,000 more homes than Shari Lewis, with her great talent and megabudget production.

The best part of this story is that when I told Ed Boland what happened, he said, "How could I cancel your show? I'd be afraid God would punish me."

Months later, however, Bordens and Coca-Cola didn't renew their options, and Vienna Sausage didn't want to shoulder all the production costs. So Jack made a deal with Bill Tarpey of Certified Food Stores, who represented 350 independent outlets. The show underwent a few changes during this period, including a new segment titled "What's New at the Zoo," which featured Dr. Lester Fisher, director of the Lincoln Park Zoo, who would bring various zoo animals down to the station. (For more on Dr. Fisher, see Chapter 13.) Jack also hired a cute seven-year-old girl to do the milk commercials, until Bill Tarpey told him to fire the "no-talent kid." Lynn-Holly Johnson, the no-talent kid in question, would go on to a successful career in the Ice Capades and have starring roles in the feature films *Ice Castles* and *For Your Eyes Only*.

Although the show's ratings climbed to 180,000 viewers, Certified dropped *The Mulqueens* in the summer of 1964. Jack recalls, "They felt that viewership declined dramatically during the summer because kids could go outside and play. They assured us that they'd pick us up again in the fall; fortunately, Vienna Sausage agreed to sponsor us for the summer." Come the fall, Vienna was out, and Certified was back in.

Jack usually avoided showing cartoons on *The Mulqueens* ("Part of it was the expense, and another reason was if the kids got hooked watching the cartoons why would they need Pandora and Mr. Hands?"), but with writer George Bloom's departure to the West Coast, they had to find new ways to hold their young viewers' attention. Throughout the 1920s, Al Christie had produced a series of silent comedy shorts. Though not as well remembered as the work of rivals Mack Sennett and Hal Roach, the Christie films were imaginative and often quite funny. The comedies—which played like live-action cartoons—could be rented cheaply enough, so Jack cut the ten-minute shorts in half and introduced "Jelly Bean Blackouts" (he and Elaine provided voices for the silent footage) as a regular feature.

During the spring of 1965, the program directors repeatedly asked Jack if he had a summer sponsor lined up. By this time, Bill Tarpey had moved up the Certified corporate ladder, and his replacement had no interest in continuing the company's association with children's programming. After much bluffing on Jack's part, *The Mulqueens* went off the air, just a little more than two years after it debuted.

"That summer was filled with appearances at Dominick's Food Stores, shopping centers, and movie theaters," remembers Jack. "When we played theaters, we were always one step ahead of the unions. We couldn't afford scale, so we'd recruit ushers, janitors, even theater managers to be stagehands. The union tried to nail us down; they'd ask us

▶ *Carson Pirie Scott department store introduces Kiddie-A-Go-Go sweatshirts to the Chicago market in 1966. (From the Mulqueen archives.)*

Mulling over their current state of affairs, Jack and Elaine huddled together and wondered where they'd wind up next. The answer came in the form of an attic at the Chicago Board of Trade.

ing a camera. To this day, I still don't know if it was our engineer's perverse idea of a practical joke or what. Jack would get upset if we made mistakes, but he also understood that our crew was not professional. And all the guys enjoyed working with Jack; they knew Jack cared, so they'd break their asses for him.

Jack and Elaine were very good about scripting and letting you know if something was going to be changed. Jack was very creative, and Elaine, of course, was the show; if something got hung up, we would tell her to stall for a couple of minutes while we got things straightened out and she always managed to come up with things that filled the time effortlessly. They even brought their "background"—we called it a "cyclorama"—which had a circus tent painted on it. We used it quite a bit as a backdrop; it ran all the way around from my control room to a door on the other side of the studio. Our cameramen overshot a lot of times, where you'd see the edge of the set and beyond. This backdrop was so expansive, if they overshot it didn't matter. It covered a lot of area and a lot of mistakes. Jack and Elaine lived and died for their show. If something got botched, it was like you stuck a knife in them.

The move to a smaller station not only lessened the show's viewership but its attractiveness to sponsors as well. Jack Mulqueen explains, "Because WCIU had a directional antenna, their broadcast signal didn't cover the Chicago area as completely as other stations did. Many people told me that they couldn't watch our show because the signal didn't come through to their part of the suburbs. Major sponsors would say to me, 'We love your show but call us when you change to another station.' But this was next to impossible since most Chicago television stations were still opposed to providing an outlet for rock-and-roll music."

Yet, as he did before, Jack managed to secure high-profile sponsors:

Every day we were on the air, we averaged about 50 to 60 children in the audience. I talked the White Castle Hamburger Company into providing meals for our audience. The only problem was that one day I wound up eating 13 hamburgers, and couldn't look at another one for a whole month.

The ironic thing about our years at Channel 26 was the fact that, because of the commission deal we had with WCIU, we were making more money during this period than we ever did at any of the bigger stations. White Castle Hamburgers and Hostess Cupcakes were two of our big sponsors.

One sponsor that didn't stay with them was the Mickelberry Meat Processing Company, though through no fault of the Mulqueens. Says Jack, "The whole company blew up—literally. One of their gas trucks was feeding into the wrong pipe and caused a combustion. A fire broke out, and the owner, the president, and the manager climbed the stairs to the roof of the building; there was a big explosion and they were all blown up."

Technical gaffes and exploding meat factories aside, *Kiddie-A-Go-Go* continued to be a favorite program of record companies. Jack explains, "The reason we remained popular with the record industry was that they didn't have many outlets for their artists who needed TV exposure. John Sipple, a promoter for Mercury Records, was in constant contact with me, and was happy to let us have anyone who was in town." The guests during this period included Glen Campbell, Roger Miller, Lesley Gore, Frankie Valli and the Four Seasons, the New Colony Six, the Blues Magoos, the Cowsills, the Left Banke, and the Hello People.

Jack recalls, "When Glen Campbell appeared on the show, he took one look at the studio and, like so many before him, was dumbfounded. He couldn't believe this was a real TV station. Roger Miller, on the other hand, didn't even know he had been booked on a kids' show. His agent neglected to inform him. So when he walked into the studio and saw our set, he yelled, 'No!' But I held up his signed contract and told him he was obligated. He yelled, 'You get one song! Just one!' He performed 'England Swings' with a scowl on his face. I remember he was out of the studio before the record even finished." Miller, like the other vocalists who appeared on the show, lipsynched to a recording. Child prodigy Ginny Tiu, who had appeared in the Elvis Presley musicals *It*

"The big stars visit Pandora at Kiddie A-Go-Go, WCIU-TV (Channel 26)"

The Flamingos

The 4 Seasons

The Left Blanke

Roger Miller

Leslie Gore, center, and Topy Malagaris, Chicago Tribune Columnist

▲ *A WCIU publicity flyer promotes the top recording artists that visited the Mulqueens' Kiddie-A-Go-Go. (From the Mulqueen archives.)*

▲ *Child star Ginny Tiu appeared on the Mulqueens'* Kiddie-A-Go-Go. *(From the Mulqueen archives.)*

Happened at the World's Fair and *Girls! Girls! Girls!,* performed on the show in a band with her brother and sister. Jack adds:

A local group called the Riddles—they had a hit song "Sweets for My Sweet"—became part of our show and appeared with us in many of the live shows we did. We once did *Kiddie-A-Go-Go* onstage at the Uptown Theater, and there were literally thousands of kids dancing in the aisles. Some members of the Riddles felt that this kiddie show exposure wasn't helping them with their teen audience, but I don't recall them complaining about any of the free publicity we got them.

Dick Clark also appeared on *Kiddie-A-Go-Go* to promote one of his movies. I couldn't blame him when he got to wciu and just stared at the place in wonderment. Elaine taught him a few go-go steps and he followed her and the kids into a Frug number. As he was leaving, I suggested we talk about the possibility of his company syndicating *Kiddie-A-Go-Go* like he did with *American Bandstand.* He didn't say anything; he just stared

not as himself but as Freckles the Clown. "The worst thing about *Clown Alley* was that clown concept," says Jackson. "It wasn't my idea to be a clown, and it hurt the show because I wasn't good at it."

Nevertheless, *Clown Alley* introduced some of Jackson's best-known creations to Chicago viewers. Dirty Dragon was still at the forefront, only now, instead of blowing powder out of his nostrils, he was rigged with tubing and smoke machines so he was actually *breathing* smoke. The technique was one of Jackson's cleverest innovations and a lasting trademark.

In addition to Morty and Fergy, and the Thumptwangers, there were Fenster the Old Professor, Mangy Lion, and the Blob. Blob was a huge mound of molding clay that Jackson shaped into an infinite variety of sizes and characters, adding different eyes, teeth, and an occasional hat. Blob never actually spoke—nothing intelligible, that is—but Jackson provided grunting sounds that would convey every emotion, from joy to outrage.

Jackson recalls:

I would try to script out things as fully as possible, but I would just write the beginning and the end of the Blob segments, and then we just went from there. We knew where we were going, or I thought I knew where we were going. We prerecorded the Blob "voices" and the work was so grueling and so demanding for the audio men. I had some excellent audio men, like Jim Shaw at WFLD.

When we'd do the Blob, I would let the audio man throw in any response he deemed appropriate . . . or inappropriate, as the case often was. They delighted in throwing me curves. If I was going to build Blob into a mountain with a stream or something like that, they had a lot of ways to be disruptive. I had a tough time getting Blob through these moments, because if he was supposed to be happy, they would delight in throwing in a sad response and I would have to ad-lib around that.

Jackson also indulged his considerable artistic abilities, drawing seasonal pictures, landscapes, still life, or, as in the case of the "I Want to

Be . . . " segments, caricatures out of a home viewer's initials. Within a matter of minutes—as a tune like the 5th Dimension's "Up, Up and Away" or Otis Redding's "Sitting on the Dock of the Bay" played in the background—he could spontaneously conjure up a piece of artwork that was both humorous and impressive.

On January 30, 1966, WBBM began airing *Here Comes Freckles*, a Sunday morning version of *Clown Alley*, taped before a live studio audience. The show never found a following, and the station pulled the plug on it on July 23, 1967.

Clown Alley limped along until August 11, 1967. "I had a certain degree of freedom," says Jackson. "But I wasn't allowed to produce the show, which I think hurt it overall. Also, it had a terrible time slot. It started five minutes *after* the half hour [6:35 A.M.] and ended five minutes *before* the hour [6:55 A.M.]. As I've said in other interviews, I was the best-kept secret in Chicago."

After the cancellation of *Clown Alley*, Jackson turned to freelance work, doing industrial films for local firms.

In 1966 Field Communications had debuted WFLD-TV, Channel 32, in Chicago. It was a new UHF (ultrahigh frequency) station, so older television sets, which were made for VHF (very high frequency) broadcasts, could not receive its signal. WFLD's first attempt to present a kid show was *Winchell and Mahoney Time*, a syndicated series starring famed ventriloquist Paul Winchell and his dummy, Jerry Mahoney. After one year, the show was dropped, and the station began looking for another children's program, this time an in-house production.

A pilot show Bill Jackson originally made for WBBM was seen by Cliff Braun, the program director of WFLD. Jackson was hired by the station, and the result was *Cartoon Town*, which debuted on February 26, 1968, sponsored by Maurice Lenell Cookies. Jackson recalls, "WFLD had this package of cartoons and needed a way to showcase them. That's where I came in. And they didn't have any preconceived ideas about what my format should be, which was great."

With *Cartoon Town*, Jackson hit his creative stride. The program's brightly colored sets were the most impressive ones ever designed for a local children's show: All the buildings, trees, furniture, and backgrounds looked as though they had come right off the pages of a comic strip or an animated cartoon. Amazingly, all this was accomplished on a slender, almost nonexistent budget.

"When it came to the sets, it helped to have an interest in art and cartooning," says Jackson. "I won't say that I designed them to the nth degree, but I certainly laid them out, so that the art directors really had a good idea of what I had in mind. And they brought their own talents to it and improved upon it."

Into these surroundings, Jackson introduced a gallery of characters that viewers fondly remember to this day. The earlier latex puppets from *The Bill Jackson Show* and *Clown Alley* were still on hand—literally—and now there was an entire town full of them: Mother Pearl Plumtree; Wally Goodscout; W.C. Cornfield; the Lemon Joke Kid; Mertz the Martian Meanie; Dr. Doompuss; Gus-Gus the Gorilla; Lila, Dirty Dragon's romantic interest; Fergy's sister Foo-Foo; a talking Suggestion Box; and Weird.

One of Jackson's most popular creations, Weird was . . . well, *weird*. With his big round eyes, flat nose, ear-to-ear smile, and unruly shock of hair, Weird was—despite a lot of competition—the wildest *Cartoon Town* character and, for many viewers, the funniest. "I based Weird on someone I knew in Chicago," says Jackson. "Of course, I'm not going to tell you who it is. But I think everyone knows someone crazy like Weird. He's essentially harmless, but definitely odd."

Wearing a derby and matching jacket, a dapper-looking Bill Jackson presided as the genial mayor of Cartoon Town, with Dirty Dragon as its smoke-blowing postmaster and Blob as the town monument. As he did with all his other shows, Jackson provided the voices for all his puppets. At director Dave Dillman's suggestion, the theme music was Sauter Finnegan's recording of "Doodletown Fifers." In was an ideal choice and gave a nice small-town feel to the opening of each program.

Jackson drew upon his youthful memories and experiences to create *Cartoon Town*, giving the show the quiet ambience of a small town, combined with the bustling activity of a carnival. This is not to imply that it was merely an overly calculated, superficial affair. On the contrary—imagination was stressed above everything else. Jackson explains:

I wanted to give as much imagination on the screen as I could. I have nothing against things like computer animation. I've seen some developments that are phenomenal. But I have to say, deep down, what I really appreciate most are things where you did a lot with very little. Let me harken back to early Jim Henson. Now, I'm not knocking the later stuff he did—he did marvelous things—but when he first started on programs like *The Ed Sullivan Show*, he did little, simple bits that were just uproarious. They were very visual and very simple.

Another act I thought was a diamond was Señor Wences. He was brilliant. I always envied him because I wound up with all these dragons and monsters and Martians. When my act comes to town, I've got a lot of luggage. And here he is with his *hand*, which he puts a little face on. Or that head in a box. Wonderful stuff. It plays on the imagination. That's what I always tried to do.

I loved the *sound* of old radio, and I always thought visually. I loved the visual effects Ernie Kovacs did; not that I copied his effects, but I wanted to do something in that spirit.

Because most viewers didn't have UHF television sets, *Cartoon Town* fought to stay on the air during its early months. Jackson relates, "WFLD was a smaller station, and no one was watching UHF. They couldn't, not without an attachment or a special set. But I knew we were onto something when I had parents come up and say, 'So you're the one! You're the one who made me go out and buy a new TV set!'"

One problem facing Jackson was the limited selection of cartoons in the station's library. For a show called *Cartoon Town*, the pickings were pretty slim. Jackson comments:

WGN bought up all the good cartoon packages. They had stuff in their library that they purchased and never even aired. WFLD didn't have that kind of money to spend, so they had to take what they could get. We had the *Out of the Inkwell* [*Koko the Clown*] cartoons and other ones that were hardly new.

For some reason, though, WGN passed on *Underdog*, and WFLD grabbed it. So I went about promoting it like it was the greatest thing since the invention of the wheel, and it became popular. We also had *Rocky and Bullwinkle* and other Jay Ward cartoons, which were all pretty funny and appealed to older viewers as well.

After a while, *Cartoon Town* began pulling in higher ratings than its chief competition, WGN's *Garfield Goose and Friends*. Jackson remembers:

We'd done very well in the afternoon against WGN. It was completely unexpected; WGN certainly didn't expect it. So they switched *Garfield Goose* to the mornings and starting throwing us up against some off-network reruns like *Batman* and *The Flintstones*. This was heavyweight stuff to try to compete with, and we didn't do as well.

WFLD pulled me out of the afternoon time slot and put me up against WGN's *Bozo's Circus* at noon, which was a mistake. That's when I changed the format. I had been doing personal appearances, stage shows with a live audience where I had people in full-sized costumes of Dirty Dragon, Mother Plumtree, and the Old Professor. So the show's title was changed to *The B.J. and Dirty Dragon Show* and I went to more of what I was doing in my stage shows. It didn't work. I realized not too far into it that this format wasn't going to make it.

So I had to go back to the front office and eat a very large portion of crow. I said, "I was wrong. This isn't working. We're having a heck of a time in the studio, but it's not being translated to the viewers at home. The fun isn't going outside the transmitter." So we went back to the old format, which made me very happy.

I was happy because, out of that experience, I got two puppeteers. I had none when I first started at WFLD, then I got one, which helped. When we went to the live audience show, I was able to get two dancers to do full-size versions of the characters

▲ *Bill Jackson and the full-sized versions of Mother Plumtree, Dirty Dragon, and the Old Professor that were seen on* The BJ and Dirty Dragon Show. *(Copyright Bill Jackson Productions. Courtesy of the Mark Yurkiw collection.)*

plus somebody to do a full-size Dirty Dragon. Out of that I got to keep one of the dancers, Nancy Wettler. Ian Harris was doing the full-size Dirty Dragon; I trained them and they trained each other. They became excellent puppeteers, especially Nancy.

I got to bring them back to the old format, and we did more serials and more musical numbers because I didn't have to have puppets on both hands and one foot!

Staying employed is quite an incentive, and that's what happened. You were not going to be employed doing shows like *Cartoon Town*. That era was coming to an end. I did try to make the transition as best as possible because I knew I wasn't going to be able to sell anybody on *Cartoon Town* or that kind of idea again.

On the other hand, I thought I could take some of the fun of *Cartoon Town*—I couldn't take it all, unfortunately—and work it into another format and make it educational or "worthwhile programming" as they called it. And I did try to put it in there the best I could. But I wanted it to be fun, because if it wasn't going to be fun, I didn't want to mess with it.

Gigglesnort Hotel debuted Sunday morning, January 5, 1975, and introduced a new character, Captain Gigglesnort, owner of the title residence. Jackson was the hotel manager, Dirty Dragon was the janitor, and the others were either guests or visitors. There was a greater emphasis on plotting, leading to thinly veiled lessons or morals, hence episodes such as "The Beauty of Silence," "Following Directions," and "Fire Safety."

Though much of the casual wackiness of *Cartoon Town* was missing, *Gigglesnort Hotel* still offered many pleasures and stands as one of Jackson's most polished productions. Says Jackson:

I had a bigger budget on *Gigglesnort*—bigger than WFLD at least—but they still didn't have much money at all. It was the smallest studio I ever worked in, yet I did the most ambitious production I've ever done in my life. We got incredible help from Dick Miller, who was the production manager, and the stagehands. Jim McPharlin, who directed the last two years of *Gigglesnort*, was a master at getting in this shoebox of a studio we had. He was excellent at space usage.

I have to tell you that the people who were working for me were really talented, and they even rose above what they had done before. [The puppeteers were Nancy Wettler and Michael Lans.] The scenery department and the prop people actually loved doing my stuff because it was such a break from what they were normally doing. They loved the imagination, they loved these wild backgrounds, and they loved being part of the show. I got a lot out of them because they were so enthused. I was very flattered when crusty old engineers were going home and telling their kids what they had done that day.

The complaint I've gotten between *Cartoon Town* and *Gigglesnort Hotel* is that some people feel *Cartoon Town* was more free-flowing and more entertaining. The interesting thing is that there were elements in *Cartoon Town* that we didn't wave a flag about, but were more on the "worthwhile" side, particularly when it came to appealing to one's imagination.

A total of 78 episodes of *Gigglesnort Hotel* were produced. The series would run for three years in syndication and reruns, winning two Chicago Emmy Awards plus a Program Director's Award for Best Locally Produced Children's Show in the nation.

Debuting on Sunday morning, August 26, 1979, on WLS, *Firehouse Follies* had the *Gigglesnort* puppets in a fire station setting. Jackson still regards this series as being vastly inferior to its predecessor. New WLS station management moved in a short time later, and the firehouse doors were sealed shut on February 17, 1980.

After *Firehouse Follies*, Bill Jackson left Chicago for the West Coast, where he joined the faculty of the California Institute for the Arts.

The impact Jackson had on Chicago children's programming and its viewers can never be overestimated. His work is still revered by his many fans. He says, "I've had some gratifying letters and conversations with people who grew up watching my shows. I don't know why they say this, but they credit me with influencing them to go on and do what they're doing in their professional lives . . . people who've gone into broadcasting, art, and other great creative endeavors."

So what is Bill Jackson's reaction when he sees some of his shows today? He replies:

My reaction? You mean when I'm not wincing? Some of the shows stand up fairly well. I'll also see scenes that don't hold up as well as I remember them. I look at *Gigglesnort Hotel* more than *Cartoon Town* because there's very little of Cartoon Town that's available.

When I watch the shows again, I generally see two things. First of all, I would like to have improved upon the pacing. For today's audience—and perhaps for the audience back then—I would like to have seen the pacing a little tighter, but I just didn't have the editing time to make it so. Secondly, I would like to have paid a little more attention to me. I'm talking about my acting. My whole thoughts were into the puppets and what they were doing. Sometimes I come off okay, and sometimes I think I'm just a piece of cardboard. I think I could have done more comedy myself and made the scenes even more fun.

As the creative force behind the programs, Bill Jackson is certainly entitled to his opinion. For the rest of us, however, watching and remembering his shows only confirms that he was one of the most inventive, most prolific, and most inspired talents in the history of Chicago television.

And we're not just blowing smoke.

Sandburg had to be pretty resourceful to come up with material for Bell to perform. (Three sketches per show, sandwiched between the cartoons.)

On one show, while Bell was introducing a military-themed Bozo cartoon, Sandburg came up with the clever idea of putting a toy army tank close to the camera lens. Thanks to forced perspective, it gave the illusion that Bell was peering out from the top of a full-sized vehicle.

Bell would often end the show by leaning back so the viewers could see the bottoms of his big floppy Bozo shoes. The bottom of the right shoe had the word *GOOD* on it, the left one had *BYE*.

Bozo ran until January 6, 1961, then was put on hiatus as WGN television and radio moved from the Tribune Tower on North Michigan Avenue to facilities on the Northwest Side at 2501 West Bradley Place, near Western and Addison. Allen Hall, who came to the station in August 1961, relates, "Before they moved to West Bradley Place, WGN shut everything down and went to very small productions. They didn't want to set up a big production and then take it down and move it. So their 1960–61 season was the season of smaller shows."

Having a larger studio to work with, WGN decided to expand the *Bozo* format and cast roster. With Bob Bell already in place as the "World's Greatest Clown,"[1] it was decided that the circus needed a ringmaster. The ideal candidate was already working at the station.

"Ned Locke was an excellent performer," says Al Hall. "He was a good person and was ideally suited for the role as ringmaster of *Bozo's Circus.*"

Born on December 25, 1919, Norbert Stoyke Locke began his career as an actor at age 16 in Oelwein, Iowa. By 1941 he was the manager of a radar factory. He later owned an aircraft agency and flying school. Locke became the Iowa State director of aeronautics and was also a staff announcer and commentator for WHO radio in Des Moines.

Locke commuted from Iowa to Chicago to produce and host WNBQ's *Uncle Ned's Squadron* (1950), billed as "an aviation program for children." During his five-year stint at WNBQ (Chicago's NBC affiliate), Locke would host children's programs like *Kids' Holiday, Sunday Funnies,* and *Captain Hartz and His Pets* (1954). In the latter, sponsored by Hartz Mountain Pet Foods, Ned played an airline pilot who traveled all over the world and showed his viewers exotic pets. He also played the district attorney on the soap opera *A Time to Live,* starred in the musical *Long Hair for Butch,* played Santa Claus on annual Christmas specials, wrote (but did not appear in) a show called *Jet Pilot,* and did commercials and weather announcements.

Locke moved to WGN in 1956 for *Lunchtime Little Theater,* a children's variety show airing weekdays at noon. (The program began in 1955; Locke joined the cast the following year.) Appearing as Uncle Ned, Locke shared hosting duties with Ted Zeigler (Uncle Bucky) and Dardanelle Hadley (Aunt Dody). William Friedkin (*The French Connection, The Exorcist*), then a staff director for the station, was one of the show's directors. Al Hall comments, "*Lunchtime Little Theater* was really the precursor of *Bozo's Circus* because it was on at noon, it had a studio audience, and they did a lot of the things we did on *Bozo:* sketches, music, cartoons, and audience games."

Ted Zeigler left *Lunchtime Little Theater* in 1959 after a contract dispute. (On the show, they explained that Uncle Bucky "stubbed his toe," supposedly behind-the-scenes shop talk for a "breakdown in contract negotiations.") Uncle Bucky was replaced by Uncle Bob, played by Bob Baron.

Zeigler tried his luck with the short-lived *Ted's Time* (1961, WMAQ), a noontime children's program featuring comedy sketches and Terrytoon cartoons. (It was doomed to fail since it aired opposite *Bozo's Circus.*) Zeigler then moved to the West Coast, where he was seen on numerous TV programs and appeared as a regular cast member on *The Hudson Brothers Razzle Dazzle Show* and *The Sonny and Cher Comedy Hour* (1971–77).

(Ted Zeigler died in 1999. Bob Baron resides in the Chicago area and is currently a member of the Senior Radio Players.)

Lunchtime Little Theater ran until 1960. Ned Locke then played Skipper Ned on *Paddleboat,* which marked the first time Locke worked with Roy Brown, who designed and operated the show's beaver puppet. Brown also provided the voice of Stokes, the unseen man in the boiler room.

During this time, Locke also served as weatherman for the *10th Hour News,* Chicago's first 30-minute nightly newscast, and Brown

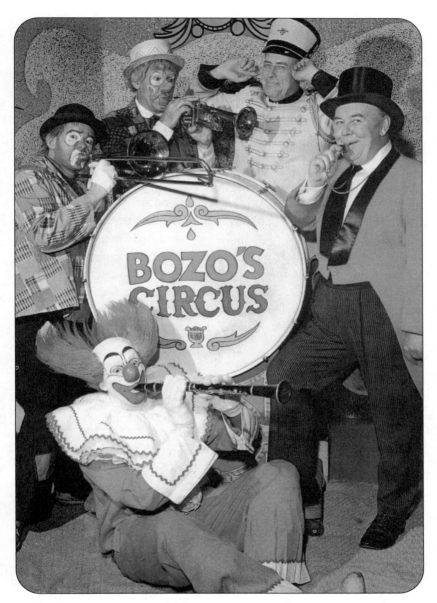

▲ *The original cast of* Bozo's Circus: *Bozo (Bob Bell), Sandy the Clown (Don Sandburg), Oliver O. Oliver (Ray Rayner), Bandleader Bob Trendler, and Ringmaster Ned Locke. (Courtesy of Don Sandburg.)*

operated the puppets on *Garfield Goose and Friends.* (For more on Brown's early career, see Chapter 6.)

When Ned Locke was cast as Ringmaster Ned for *Bozo's Circus,* *Paddleboat* ended its one-year run. On the final installment, Skipper Ned received a big carton containing his ringmaster's uniform and explained to the viewers that he was now going to work for the circus. These kinds of transitions were quite common with the station's programming policy. Al Hall observes, "WGN always had the idea that this stuff was real for kids, so they always provided an explanation for any changes."

Bob Trendler, WGN's musical director, was the obvious choice for the leader of the Big Top Band, also known as the WGN Orchestra. Trendler started with WGN radio in 1935 and had been involved with the station's television broadcasts since 1948. Al Hall explains, "The station had Bob under union contract and they had to pay him whether they used him or not. So when they came up with *Bozo's Circus* they decided to use him for that. Oh, his band was great! And Bob himself was a good addition to the show; he played the part of the maestro very well."

Hall was also added to the mix as the show's director: "I had been working in Indianapolis and I heard there was an opening at WGN. So I talked to the person in charge of hiring and came to the station on August 28, 1961. My first assignment was *Bozo's Circus."*

Bozo's Circus *is on the air!*
 — Ringmaster Ned

The one-hour edition of *Bozo's Circus* debuted at noon on Monday, September 11, 1961, live from WGN's Studio One. Before a studio audience of more than 200 people (always referred to as "a cast of thousands"), Ned Locke introduced the program as Bob Trendler and his 13-piece Big Top Band played the theme from *The Greatest Show on Earth* (1952), the Academy Award–winning circus film directed by Cecil B. DeMille.

With a bigger studio and considerable ballyhoo, the show seemed to have everything going for it, except for one major ingredient: Bozo. A budgeting error by producer Jim McGinn resulted in the program not

his time desperately trying to keep his three wild clowns in line. Bozo, he's a bedeviling, aggressive type person who's always the perennial wise guy. Nevertheless, he was a lovable character. Now, we needed someone who is kind of gullible, who goes along with everything, and usually ends up on the short end of the stick. [Oliver was always on the losing end of Bozo's "fair-square" contests.] And a country bumpkin seemed to be the perfect role, a buffoon for Bozo to play off of. So that's the way Ray ended up. Bozo liked to play tricks on me as well. But I always came out pretty much on top. I think we had a varied foursome. Kids liked me as a mute clown. They felt sorry for me because I couldn't communicate, and a lot of kids that age don't communicate well either and could identify with me.

Much of the dialogue went over the younger viewers' heads. But that was okay. I feel that a child should "reach up" to the material, because that's the way he or she learns.

Oliver wore a rubber nose. I believe Roy Brown made it for him. Ray, who already had a sizable nose, would occasionally forget to wear his rubber nose, but few people noticed the difference. Wimpy helped him with his makeup. I cast Oliver as a country bumpkin from a fictitious town called Puff Bluff, Kentucky, about which I later wrote a song for Oliver to sing.

The Chicago edition of *Bozo's Circus* proved to be hugely popular with viewers. In time, WGN announced there was a ten-year waiting list for tickets. The demand was so great that news services reported stories about expectant mothers and engaged couples sending away for tickets in advance, to make sure their unborn children would have the opportunity of seeing the show.

Bozo Myth #2

Although there was a demand for Bozo tickets, the hype was also a publicity gimmick. Jack Mulqueen remembers, "When we were doing our show The Mulqueens *at WGN, I was approached by Helen Reise, who ran the Grey Line Bus Tours. Knowing that we had an audience of 200 families attending our show each week, she tried to convince me to have a bus pick them up and bring them to the station. We had an arrange-*

ment where people picked up ticket applications for our show at sponsor's stores, like Certified Grocers. This was a great marketing tool, one that made it impossible to arrange for a bus tour.

"However, I found out from Helen just how Bozo's Circus *guaranteed its large audience. For the first year or two* Bozo *was on, their audience consisted of kids being bused in from local schools, not families who wrote in for tickets. As the demand for* Bozo *tickets grew, Helen was given a smaller number of children to bus to the show. This explains why* Bozo *was booked so many years in advance."*

The popularity of *Bozo's Circus* resulted in an evening edition of the show, the aforementioned *Big Top*, which aired Wednesdays at 6:30 P.M. Mark Yurkiw notes, "*Big Top* consisted primarily of taped highlights from the regular daily series. There were no cartoons. There was a new Grand Prize Game, but with a twist: The parents participated in the contest, taking over in the event the child missed one of the buckets." *Big Top* debuted in 1965 and ended its run in 1967. (From 1967 to 1970 WGN would also rebroadcast *Bozo's Circus* on Saturdays at noon, although it never fared as well in the ratings as it did in its weekday time slot.)

Although he would later turn down offers, Bob Bell made a handful of personal appearances as Bozo, including a 45-minute performance by the cast at the 34th Chicagoland Music Festival at Soldier Field in 1963. There were also numerous *Bozo* TV specials, such as *Bozo's Christmas* (1962), taped at Medinah Temple; *Bozo's Holiday Circus* (1963), taped at the Arie Crown Theater; and the 1979 and 1980 *Bozo's Circus* broadcasts from the annual ChicagoFest.

In 1967 Don Sandburg was also seen as a mute Ronald McDonald in a series of Chicago television commercials for the McDonald's franchise. The following year, he planned to leave Chicago for the West Coast around Christmas. But when Bob Bell underwent surgery for a brain aneurysm, Sandburg decided to stay a couple more months. As he explained to Mark Yurkiw, "When Bob ended up in the hospital, that left just two clowns, Oliver and myself. We needed a third person, so I used my floor director, Dick Lubbers, as a replacement and named him Monty Melvin, the carnival barker. I borrowed the name from a schoolmate of mine. I always thought he had a catchy showbiz type name, so I gave it to Lubbers for his clown name. So there we were, the four of us: Ringmaster Ned, Oliver, Monty, and me."

That year two new clowns began making intermittent appearances on the show: Roy Brown as Cooky the Cook and Marshall Brodien as Wizzo the Wizard. Both would eventually become regular cast members.

A graduate of Austin High School and a commercial art student at the School of the Art Institute and the Chicago Academy of Fine Arts, Roy Brown was an invaluable behind-the-scenes talent at WGN. His puppetry and artwork were familiar to viewers of programs like *Garfield Goose and Friends, Ray Rayner and His Friends,* and *Family Classics.* After more than a decade at the station, Brown had his first real on-camera role as Cooky.

As Brown told Jim Mueller, "I'd been writing scripts for *Bozo* on the side and told Don [Sandburg] I wanted to audition for the clown part. Bozo and Oliver O. Oliver had a running gag about lousy circus food, but they, of course, meant the food in our WGN cafeteria. It was a great

▸ *Roy Brown as Cooky the Clown on the set of* Bozo's Circus *(1967, WGN). (Courtesy of Don Sandburg.)*

inside joke. Anyway, I decided the circus needed a cook to play off them and their smart remarks, and that's where Cooky came from."

Brown devised his own clown makeup and even went into the WGN prop room and took one of the Bozo wigs, which he cut down for his character. As Cooky, Brown was a solid addition to the show.

Al Hall reflects, "Roy was an old vaudevillian—that's the best way I can describe him. He knew all the old routines because, like Bob Bell, he had been a 'naughty boy' during his school years and he often found himself in one or two burlesque theaters, cheering on the sundry comics. So he knew all the stuff and was a pretty good improviser. He and Bob Bell worked together like two gloves. I swear to God that they could read each other's mind. Roy was never a comic competitor with Bob, or later with Joey D'Auria. Roy knew he was the 'second banana' and played the part perfectly."

Brown considered a sketch called "Pure Imagination" to be the finest bit he ever did on the show. He later told writer Jim Mueller, "Bob and Ned wanted no part of 'Pure Imagination.' They sat and scowled the first time we rehearsed, because 'Pure Imagination' was such a departure for Bozo. 'Pure Imagination' had Bozo dancing with this doll and Cooky looking on longingly. Bozo leaves, and Cooky's left alone, sitting on a bucket with a mop, all forlorn, absently stroking the mop head like it's the girl of his dreams. Cooky begins to dance with the mop, he twirls behind a pillar and when he reappears, the mop is a real girl. There are no lines, it's all pantomime."

Al Hall remembers one more aspect of this sketch, which he related to Mueller: "Bozo came roaring across the stage, dancing with a life-size Raggedy Ann doll, and the doll's bloomers fell down around its ankles. The audience and the clowns laughed for a solid three minutes on that one."

As Wizzo, "the World's Wackiest Wizard" (his magic chant, "Doody-Doody-Doo," became his trademark), Marshall Brodien also made valuable contributions to the program. Al Hall comments, "Marshall first appeared on the show in 1962, and we had a policy that we would never bring a guest act back more than twice a year. In his first year, Marshall was on the show 22 times. He was just so good, a very engaging talent and he made solid contributions. The thing I liked about

Al Hall later told writer and historian Keith Stras, "I really missed Ned when he left because he was the person around whom the *Bozo* show flowed. Although it was *Bozo's Circus*, it more rightfully might have been called *Ned's Circus* because Ned did all the commercials, he did the Grand Prize Game, he did the audience game, he introduced everything, he was the locus around which this whole thing revolved. Ned was always the calming force and he maintained a very dignified presentation."

Upon retiring, Ned Locke sold his home in Wheaton, Illinois, and his ranch in Colorado and moved to his dream house in Kimberling City, Missouri. There he went into real estate and became the park commissioner, the police commissioner, and finally the mayor.

Frazier Thomas took over as the host of *Bozo* on July 27, 1976, although *Garfield Goose and Friends* continued to air as a separate program until September 10, 1976. Al Hall recalls, "Frazier was a good performer, but he was concerned about all the impromptu stuff we did. He was used to being prepared and in control. I think he adapted to working methods very well, although they were the polar opposite of his working methods."

Thomas was often at a loss to cope with the show's improvisational, free-for-all approach. During one 1978 broadcast, the cast bombarded an unsuspecting Thomas with shaving cream pies. He simply stood there, immobile, as the clowns gleefully pelted him from head to toe.

In 1979 Thomas described his working conditions to radio personality Ed Schwartz:

> When we go into the first meeting, everybody will toss an idea into the pot and by the time that meeting is over, everything has been changed. It took me a long while to get used to that. I'm the only one who gets a script ahead of time, so I had my part all marked. I know exactly what I was supposed to do because I have always liked to know what I was going to do before I did it. Now, that doesn't bother them a bit but it does bother me.
>
> I was the new boy on the block so I said, "Give me the script at least an hour ahead of time so I know what I'm going to do and I can sort of plan it out." By the time we had been through the first meeting, the script had been changed. I go around then

to rehearsal and by that time the script was changed again. And by the time we get it on the air, they may not have done it the same way we rehearsed it the second time. Al Hall says, "You've got to be flexible." I said, "Flexible? This is ridiculous!"

After three years, it's easier. I look at things and shake my head sometimes and say, "Man, that's not the way we did it in rehearsal at all." And Al says, "No, it came off fine, everything went fine." I'd say, "You've got to be out of your mind! I didn't know what we were doing!"

In regard to his five-minute Garfield Goose segments on *Bozo*, Thomas remarked, "I miss the kinds of things that I could do for the youngsters, at least the kind of things that I thought contributed to their entertainment. I don't have the time to do those things now. It's not the same kind of a show. I mean, this is a circus show that has to move fast and keep moving. It's a different type of entertainment. I miss what I thought contributed to the youngsters' imaginations and things that I could only do on [*Garfield Goose and Friends*]." (For more on Frazier Thomas, see Chapter 6.)

In the summer of 1980, *Bozo's Circus* became *The Bozo Show*. It was switched from noon to a weekday morning (8 A.M.) time slot and was no longer aired live. More changes followed.

Starting January 26, 1981, *The Bozo Show* was seen weekday mornings from 7 to 8:30 A.M., in the old *Ray Rayner and His Friends* time slot. The *Garfield Goose* puppets were dropped entirely, as Cuddley Dudley—a staple of Rayner's show—took their place. The familiar *Greatest Show on Earth* opening theme was replaced by an instrumental version of a station promo song. The circus was replaced by a circular stage, effectively eliminating the Grand March finale. Additional cartoons took the place of circus acts. And, in a bow to modern technology, the Magic Arrows were dropped in favor of the Bozoputer as a way of selecting contestants for the Grand Prize Game. As more than one veteran viewer remarked, "This is progress? Give me the good old days!"

When the 90-minute format was adopted, so were new working methods. At this point, WGN would tape six shows a week (one in the morning, one in the afternoon, on Mondays, Tuesdays, and Wednesdays) from September through April. Five of the six shows would be aired the following week, and the sixth one would be held for broadcast later in the season (reruns were broadcast during the summer). Frequently, the final show, as aired, would include segments taped on different days.

By 1983 *The Bozo Show* returned to using its original opening theme and added Pat Hurley to the cast. Hurley, who was previously seen on the ABC-TV children's program *Kids Are People Too*, interviewed youngsters in the studio audience and often did the preshow warm-up. There were also reports that Bob Bell, Bozo himself, intended to retire at the end of the 1983–84 season.

In 1984 a brand-new set replaced the ill-conceived circular stage, allowing the much-missed Grand March to resume.

On Wednesday, April 4, 1984, Bob Bell taped his final *Bozo* show. The last comedy sketch was a pie fight free-for-all, ending Bell's tenure with a bang.

Four days later, on Sunday, April 8, WGN aired *Bozo: The Man Behind the Makeup*, a lovingly crafted career tribute written and hosted by newscaster Denise Cannon. "I've worked with a lot of actors," Ray Rayner said on the program. "I consider Bob Bell one of the finest comedy actors I've ever worked with. We did everything you can think of: vaudeville, old burlesque bits, slapstick out of the movies. Every one you could think of, we did, and oriented it towards the *Bozo* show. And, of course, the key was Bob Bell."

Most viewers were unaware of the fact that throughout his years as Bozo, Bob Bell maintained his status as a WGN staff announcer, doing the station's early morning news and weather reports. As Frazier Thomas commented to Ed Schwartz, "He gets here at 5 or 5:30 and signs on the station every morning. I said, 'Bob, I don't understand you. You don't have to do this. Why do you want to be a staff man?' And he says, 'You never can tell how long this Bozo thing is going to last. I want a staff job to fall back on.'" When Denise Cannon inquired, Bell explained, "Because nothing is forever in radio or television. The huge success today could be the afterthought of tomorrow."

In the show's closing moments, Bell put everything into perspective:

"There's nothing I would have done differently because, looking back now, this is about as fulfilling as anybody's job could be. You're involved with nothing but happiness. There are no sad times, particularly. So to be involved in happiness and laughter as a livelihood is like a vacation every day. And I won't forget that."

Also in 1984, the Chicago chapter of the National Academy of Television Arts and Sciences board of directors presented Bell with a Governors Award, its highest honor. Considering Bell's sly sense of humor, no doubt he would have been equally proud to have learned that Chicago native Dan Castellaneta patterned his vocal characterization of Krusty the Clown on *The Simpsons* after Bell's portrayal of Bozo.

Bob and his wife, Carol, moved to San Diego. He said he would do "absolutely nothing" now that he was retired and often joked that he would get up every morning and compose a "Things Not to Do" list. But a man with Bell's enthusiasm and interest in people couldn't remain idle for long, so in addition to presiding over the local Kiwanis Club, he became involved with community and fund-raising endeavors.

With Bob Bell's departure, the main question was now who would—or could—replace a man who had become a Chicago institution?

After a three-month nationwide talent search, Joey D'Auria, a stand-up comedian and a graduate of the American Academy of Dramatic Arts, was selected to fill Bell's oversized shoes. D'Auria taped his first *Bozo* show on Wednesday, September 5, 1984. To several generations of fans, Bell was the one-and-only Bozo, and no one could ever hope to take his place. However, D'Auria brought a new energy and persona to the role. Wisely, he never tried to imitate Bell. Instead, D'Auria's Bozo was cheerier and a lot less cantankerous, although he was still full of mischief and wasn't above pulling practical jokes on his cohorts. Al Hall says, "Joey's a good artist and he changed the Bozo makeup slightly so that it suited him better. Joey also made a lot of personal appearances as Bozo. Bob Bell never really cared to make personal appearances, but Joey was pleased to do them because he real-

Also in 1994, *The Bozo Show* lost its weekday morning time slot. Al Hall says, "WGN took *Bozo* off five days a week and installed a news program because they wanted to sell commercials that appealed to adults." Rechristened *The Bozo Super Sunday Show*, this two-hour edition (8 to 10 A.M.) was actually two different shows with two different audiences aired back-to-back. To help ease ticket demand, summer reruns were abandoned in favor of new shows. To make up for the loss of Roy Brown, Marshall Brodien, and Michael Immel (who also left in 1994), *The Bozo Super Sunday Show* added Robin Eurich as Rusty the Handyman (1994–2001), Cathy Schenkelberg as Pepper (1994–96), and Michele Gregory as 'Tunia (1994–98) to its roster of clowns.

In 1995 the show returned to a 60-minute format (8 to 9 A.M.), bringing back the Bozo cartoons, which had not been telecast on a regular basis after the 1982–83 season. During the 1995–96 and 1996–97 seasons, the Bozo cartoons were featured on every show.

For the 1996–97 season, *Bozo* celebrated its 35th anniversary. Roy Brown came back as Cooky for the first show of the season (aired September 8, 1996) and a weekly "Best of Bozo" segment (utilizing old clips) was featured.

In 1997 the show moved to a 7 A.M. time slot and, in compliance with an FCC ruling to provide viewers with more educational content, stopped airing cartoons.

After a lengthy illness, Bob Bell died of a heart attack on December 8, 1997, in San Marcos, California. He was eulogized in newspaper editorials as a genuine television pioneer and one of the industry's most-beloved performers. In honor of the man who many viewers felt was truly the "World's Greatest Clown," a section of West Addison Street between Western Avenue and the Chicago River was named Bob Bell Way.

In 1998 Joey D'Auria won a Chicago Emmy Award for his work on *The Bozo Super Sunday Show*.

On October 25, 2000, a very frail Roy Brown made a surprise guest appearance as Cooky on what turned out to be the last new installment of *The Bozo Super Sunday Show* (it was aired on December 31, 2000). Al Hall appeared as the Circus Boss, and everyone joined in on a big pie fight. Brown, as Cooky, led the Grand March finale.

On January 22, 2001, Roy Thomas Brown died of congestive heart failure at the Alexian Brothers Medical Center in Elk Grove Village, Illinois. Joey D'Auria told Dean Richards, "When I visited Roy in the hospital before he passed away, one of the last things he said was, 'I really don't have any regrets. I'm one of the few people who can say that I spent my life doing what I loved.'"

The future of *Bozo* looked bleak. Joey D'Auria suspected something was up in January 2001 when WGN was reluctant to pay for the annual cleaning of the Bozo wig. On March 23, 2001, WGN vice president and general manager John Vitanovec announced the *Bozo* show would be canceled after a mind-boggling four decades on the air. In a *Chicago Tribune* article titled "Kids' Shows No Longer Send in the Clowns" (Wednesday, March 28, 2001), Steve Johnson reported Vitanovec felt that *Bozo* no longer fit the station's image as a producer of local news and sports programs: "I can only ask that the fans of *Bozo* know that we don't make this decision lightly. Every decision's a business decision but that doesn't make this one any easier . . . my son may not like to be the son of the father who did away with *Bozo*."

In a *Chicago Sun-Times* article titled "Send Out the Clown: WGN Ends Bozo's Circus" (Saturday, March 24, 2001), media columnist Robert Feder quoted Joey D'Auria's reaction: "Shows like *Bozo* aren't being done anymore. The fact that WGN continued doing this show and had such a strong feeling for the character and for the community was very important. But in today's market, it was a bit of a dinosaur."

The final show, a 90-minute special titled *Bozo: 40 Years of Fun!* (taped Tuesday, June 12, 2001; aired Saturday, July 14, 2001) starred Joey D'Auria, Robin Eurich, and Andy Mitran, with former cast members Don Sandburg and Marshall Brodien. Special musical guests were Billy Corgan and Jimmy Chamberlin (Smashing Pumpkins), Eddie "King" Roeser (Urge Overkill), Chris Holmes, and Linda Strawberry.

Still incensed over the cancellation, Robert Feder took the station to task in a *Chicago Sun-Times* article titled "Why Barbarians Killed Bozo" (Friday, July 13, 2001): "The way the folks at WGN-Channel 9 have been carrying on about this weekend's *Bozo* special, you'd never know they're the barbarians responsible for killing Chicago's favorite clown and destroying a beloved television institution. . . . In reality, all the hype and all the spin are designed to divert attention from the fact that Channel 9 bosses deliberately sabotaged the longest-running and most revered children's show in local television history. Why? So they could make it disappear without much uproar and goose their bottom line by a few hundred thousand bucks. . . . What a shame. Even a clown deserves a decent funeral."

Reruns of *The Bozo Super Sunday Show* were broadcast until August 26, 2001. At that point, the last remaining tie to Chicago's golden age of children's television was officially severed.

The phenomenal success of Chicago's *Bozo's Circus* stands as a testament to the talented members of its cast and crew. There has never been another show like it—and, in this era of disposable entertainment, there never will be.

1. According to Jim Mueller, famed clown Emmett Kelly reportedly threatened legal action over the use of his "World's Greatest Clown" title. So Bozo became the "World's Most Famous Clown" sometime around 1970.

throughout the screening. He would also do stunts and comedy bits that, while silly to adults, were hilarious to children.

An energetic performer who was always eager to please his faithful followers, Coons parlayed the success of *Noontime Comics* into another program, *Life with Johnny Coons* (1954–55, WBBM) and a network version of *Noontime Comics* called *The Uncle Johnny Coons Show* (1956).

Eleven-year-old Susan Heinkel starred in *Susie's Show*, a still-impressive program that debuted in 1956 on WBBM. A native of St. Louis, Missouri, Heinkel was discovered in a St. Louis Christmas pageant when she was three years old and had starred in *Suzy's Playroom* for a local St. Louis station. By the time she arrived in Chicago, Heinkel was completely at ease in front of the camera, possessing a natural poise and charm that made her one of the most appealing young television performers of this or any other era.

True to the show's title, Heinkel's character was the main focus of the program. She would sit on a magic flying stool, and by repeating a magic chant ("I wish there were a land of play, I wish that I could fly away"), she and her terrier, Rusty, would be whisked off to a fantasyland called Wonderville. Surrounded by oversized props, Susan would sing songs, converse with a talking table named Mr. Pegasus and the top-hatted Caesar P. Penguin (both voiced by John Coughlin), and interact with novelty and animal acts, while a convenient Cartoon-a-Machine conjured up whatever animated shorts were currently in the station's film library. (Popeye cartoons were featured when the show aired locally; Terrytoons were featured when the show went network.) The talented Miss Heinkel proved to be a lively and resourceful host during these live telecasts; often, when Rusty missed a cue, Susan was able to ad-lib her way out of situations that would have produced flop sweat in the most seasoned adult performers.

In 1957 *Susie's Show* became *Susan's Show* when it was picked for a CBS network slot. Heinkel won a Chicago Emmy Award in 1958. The following year, the show was retitled *Susan and the Professor*, presumably to avoid confusion with the CBS sitcom *Susie*, starring Ann Sothern.

After *Susan and the Professor* was canceled in 1959, Susan Heinkel starred in *Teenland*, which contained elements of her earlier program.

▶ *Pandora's go-go costume from the Mulqueens'* Kiddie-A-Go-Go *on display at the Museum of Broadcast Communications. (From the Mulqueen archives.)*

Ray Rayner, Bill Jackson, John Conrad, Don Sandburg, and Marshall Brodien were all there to take their well-deserved bows. A little grandmother walked up to me and said, "Hi! I'm Mary Hartline." As I looked around the room I noticed it was filled with senior citizens. And I was one of them.

It was exciting to be recognized for my accomplishments, but there was something missing: Elaine. She deserved to be part of this event, but her health prohibited her attendance. So, for me, the day felt incomplete.

☆   ☆   ☆

MARSHALL BRODIEN has marketed and produced television commercials and continues representing and packaging magic kits for famed illusionists Siegfried and Roy. Brodien also created a magic kit that was part of the merchandising for Disney Pictures' *Aladdin* (1992). He currently resides in Illinois.

After moving to the West Coast in 1969, JOHN CONRAD bought a Dollar-a-Day car rental franchise. After about four years, he bought a coffee machine business, then he went into the air filtration business with Alpine Air Purification Systems of Los Angeles. He is currently the president of Global Consumer Services, Inc.

After her retirement, MARY HARTLINE kept busy with numerous social events and charity fund-raising. She currently resides in Illinois.

BILL JACKSON moved to the West Coast, where he cut a pilot for a series called *Le Hot Spot*, about two rival nightclubs. "The concept was that these dragons were opening a new nightclub, which didn't sit well with Big Al, played by Broderick Crawford, who was already operating one. The pilot was terrible and it never sold."

▼ *An oil painting of* Cartoon Town *and its characters, by Bill Jackson. (Courtesy of Bill Jackson.)*

ble, even sluggish, stream in the right place at the right time. That's the story of the making of Chicago. This is the other story—the story of the making and perpetual re-making of a river by everything from geological forces to the interventions of an emerging and mighty city. Winner of an American Regional History Publishing Award: 1st Place—Midwest, 2001; winner of the 2000 Midwest Independent Publishers Association Award: Merit Award (2nd Place) in History.
1-893121-02-x, August 2000, softcover, 302 pages, 78 photos, $16.95

Great Chicago Fires:
Historic Blazes That Shaped a City
David Cowan
Acclaimed author (*To Sleep with the Angels*) and veteran firefighter David Cowan tells the story of the other "great" Chicago fires, noting the causes, consequences, and historical context of each—from the burning of Fort Dearborn in 1812 to the Iroquois Theater disaster to the Our Lady of the Angels school fire.
1-893121-07-0, July 2001, softcover, 10" x 8", 167 pages, 86 historic photos, $19.95

The Firefighter's Best Friend: Lives and Legends of Chicago
Firehouse Dogs
Trevor Orsinger and Drew Orsigner
Working dogs are an often-overlooked segment of the canine population. The *Firefighter's Best Friend* provides a rare look into a specific type of these dogs-those who have lived or currently live in the firehouses of Chicago. The Orsinger brothers take readers on a tour of Chicago firehouses in their quest to document the lives and legends of every known Chicago firedog past and present. As seen in *Dog & Kennel, Dog World*, and *Animal Fair* magazines, the *Chicago Sun-Times*, the *Chicago Tribune*, and in the popular *Dogs with Jobs* television series.
1-893121-20-8, September 2003, softcover, 11" x 8.5", 163 pages, 152 historic and contemporary photos, $19.95.

Graveyards of Chicago:
The People, History, Art, and Lore of Cook County Cemeteries
Matt Hucke and Ursula Bielski
Ever wonder where Al Capone is buried? How about Clarence Darrow? Muddy Waters? Harry Caray? And what really lies beneath home plate at Wrigley Field? *Graveyards of Chicago* answers these and other cryptic questions as it charts the lore and lure of Chicago's ubiquitous burial grounds. Grab a shovel and tag along as Ursula Bielski and Matt Hucke unearth the legends and legacies that mark Chicago's silent citizens.
0-9642426-4-8, November 1999, softcover, 228 pages, 168 photos, $15

Literary Chicago: A Book Lover's Tour of the Windy City
By Greg Holden, with foreword by Harry Mark Petrakis
Chicago has attracted and nurtured writers, editors, publishers, and book lovers for more than a century and continues to be one of the nation's liveliest literary cities. Join Holden as he journeys through the streets, people, ideas, events, and culture of Chicagoland's historic and contemporary literary world. Includes 11 detailed walking/driving tours.
1-893121-01-1, March 2001, softcover, 332 pages, 83 photos, 11 maps, $15.95

Hollywood on Lake Michigan: 100 Years of Chicago and the Movies
Arnie Bernstein, foreword by Soul Food writer/director George Tillman, Jr.
Tours, trivia, special articles, historic and contemporary photos, film profiles, anecdotes, and exclusive interviews with dozens of personalities spotlight Chicago and Chicagoans' distinguished role in cinematic history. Winner of an American Regional History Publishing Award: 1st Place—Midwest, 2000!
0-9642426-2-1, December 1998, softcover, 364 pages, 80 photos, $15

Local Ghostlore

Chicago Haunts: Ghostlore of the Windy City
Ursula Bielski
From ruthless gangsters to restless mail order kings, from the Fort Dearborn Massacre to the St. Valentine's Day Massacre, the phantom remains of the passionate people and volatile events of Chicago history have made the Second City second to none in the annals of American ghostlore. Bielski captures over 160 years of this haunted history with her unique blend of lively storytelling, in-depth historical research, exclusive interviews, and insights from parapsychology. Called "a masterpiece of the genre," "a must-read," and "an absolutely first-rate-book" by reviewers, Chicago Haunts continues to earn the praise of critics and readers alike. Our best-seller!
0-9642426-7-2, October 1998, softcover, 277 pages, 29 photos, $15

More Chicago Haunts: Scenes from Myth and Memory
Ursula Bielski
Chicago. A town with a past. A people haunted by its history in more ways than one. A "windy city" with tales to tell . . . Bielski is back with more history, more legends, and more hauntings, including the personal scary stories of *Chicago Haunts* readers. A new favorite!
1-893121-04-6, October 2000, softcover, 312 pages, 50 photos, $15

Creepy Chicago: A Ghosthunter's Tales of the City's Scariest Sites
Ursula Bielski; illustrations by Amy Noble
Nineteen illustrated stories for readers ages 8–12 delve into Chicago's famous phantoms, haunted history, and unsolved mysteries, including Resurrection